TANTRIC TREASURES

TANTRIC TREASURES

Three Collections of Mystical Verse

from Buddhist India

INTRODUCED, TRANSLATED, AND ANNOTATED BY

Roger R. Jackson

OXFORD
UNIVERSITY PRESS

2004

OXFORD
UNIVERSITY PRESS

Oxford New York
Auckland Bangkok Buenos Aires Cape Town Chennai
Dar es Salaam Delhi Hong Kong Istanbul Karachi Kolkata
Kuala Lumpur Madrid Melbourne Mexico City Mumbai Nairobi
São Paulo Shanghai Taipei Tokyo Toronto

Published by Oxford University Press, Inc.
198 Madison Avenue, New York, New York 10016

www.oup.com

Library of Congress Cataloging-in-Publication Data
Tantras. Selections. English.
Tantric treasures : three collections of mystical verse from Buddhist India / introduced, translated, and annotated by Roger R. Jackson.
p. cm.
Includes bibliographical references.
ISBN 0-19-516640-X; 0-19-516641-8 (pbk.)
I. Sarahapāda, 8th cent. Dohākoṣa. II. Kṛṣṇavajrapāda, 11th cent. Dohākoṣa. III. Tillopāda, 988–1069. Dohākoṣa. IV. Jackson, Roger R. V. Title.
PK1428.T36 Z9 2004
294.3'82—dc22 2003022680

9 8 7 6 5 4 3 2 1

Printed in the United States of America
on acid-free paper

Preface

The purpose of this book is to provide an accurate and, I hope, accessible and poetically interesting translation of three classics of medieval Indian Buddhist mysticism, the Apabhraṃśa-language *Dohākoṣas* ("Treasuries of Couplets") of the great tantric masters Saraha, Kāṇha, and Tilopa. As the best mystical texts do, these collections combine first-person reports of the author's experience, attempts to describe an indescribable ultimate, and advice on what to do—and what not to do—in order to experience that ultimate oneself. All three texts have been translated into Western languages before. Saraha's *Treasury* has been translated at least four times, into French by Muhammad Shahidullah (1928), into English by David Snellgrove (1954), into English (though from the Tibetan rather than the Apabhraṃśa version) by Herbert Guenther (1993), and into English (again from Tibetan) by Kurtis Schaeffer (2000, unpublished). Kāṇha's *Treasury* has been translated once, into French by Shahidullah (1928). Tilopa's *Treasury* has been translated twice, by N. N. Bhattacharyya (1982) and (from the Tibetan) Fabio Torricelli (1997). These renditions have been made by scholars who are excellent philologists and/or philosophers and whose primary interest, therefore, was in precision rather than poetry. Yet the Treasuries are deeply poetic texts, rooted in vernacular north Indian song styles of the late first millennium C.E., and replete with mystery, humor, paradox, and profundity, all conveyed with a refreshing, aphoristic directness. They have influenced poetry and song—not to mention spiritual life—in India, Nepal, and Tibet for a thousand years, and resonate as well with mystical verse from elsewhere, whether by Rumi, or Blake, or Kerouac and Ginsberg. They are great enough, and important enough, that, like the classics of both East and West, they can be mined repeatedly by translators, and their riches will never be exhausted.

I have been interested in Saraha, Kāṇha, and Tilopa for many years now, for they are important influences on Tibetan Buddhist traditions that long have preoccupied me, both personally and as a scholar. As part of my study of the ideas and practices surrounding the "great seal" (*mahāmudrā*) in India and Tibet, I have been reading the three Treasuries in various languages, Asian and Western, for nearly a quarter century, trying with each reading (and in occasional writings) to draw closer and closer to the nub of what their charismatic, elusive authors were trying to say—about the world, the mind, and how to live in an enlightened way. Without in the least intending to denigrate previous translations—from which, in fact, I have benefited immeasurably—I thought there was room still for a version of the three Treasuries that sought to bring to them a more contemporary poetic sensibility, without extracting them entirely from the cultural world from which they arose. I am not much of a poet (let alone a philologist or a philosopher), but I do love poetry enough that I could not resist attempting to carry across to readers of English something of my own sense of what these three figures may have conveyed to their original audiences, and convey today to their Asian descendants and to us. Experts in Indian, Buddhist, or tantric studies will find little new in my introduction or annotations, but I do hope that they, like the interested members of the educated public for whom this has been written, will find something of value in my renditions of the dohās, and in my attempts to locate them, difficult as it is to do so, in time, place, culture, and religion.

Besides the pioneering scholars just mentioned, I have learned a great deal over the years about these poets, their songs, and their context from conversations with (and the work of) my great friends from graduate school, John and Beth Newman, José Cabezón, and John Makransky, and a number of scholars I have had the fortune to know since, most notably Luis Gómez, Janet Gyatso, Donald Lopez, Matthew Kapstein, Ronald Davidson, Dan Martin, and Kurtis Schaeffer. Looming behind them all as a constant, open-minded presence is my mentor, Geshe Lhundub Sopa, professor emeritus at the University of Wisconsin. In developing an approach to translating Asian poetry, I have read, enjoyed, and been influenced by the efforts of a great many predecessors, including A. K. Ramanujan, Edward Dimock and Denise Levertov, Dilip Chitre, Robert Bly, Linda Hess and Shukdev Singh, Andrew Schelling, Stephan Beyer, Glenn Mullin, Rick Fields, Gary Snyder, Kenneth Rexroth, Burton Watson, Sam Hamill, W. S. Merwin, and the radical *adiguru* of them all, Ezra Pound, from whom I have stolen the initial "Bah!" of my translation of Saraha's first verse. Of continuing inspiration over the years in matters poetic have been my word-bedazzled friends Dan Bromberg, Frank Levering, Erin McMahon, Sue Solomon, and Wendy King, and, though they now, and all too soon, are past where words can reach, Harvey Sacks and Marion Percy. As I brought the manuscript toward completion, I received great encouragement from my colleagues in the Religion department at Carleton College, and valuable advice and assistance from Cynthia Read, Theo Calderara, Heather Hartman, and Jessica Ryan of Oxford University Press. I am also grateful to Oxford's anonymous readers, whose comments, criticisms, and suggestions I have found both perceptive and useful.

As always, my greatest supports—and support, as any writer knows, may include not just encouraging one's efforts but dragging one off on occasion for a game of catch or to smell the new blossomed lilies—have been my son, Ian Jackson, and my wife, Pam Percy, to whom this is lovingly dedicated.

Contents

Abbreviations

Apa.	=	Apabhraṃśa
B	=	P. C. Bagchi (1938), *Dohakoṣa*
G	=	H. V. Guenther (1993), *Ecstatic Spontaneity*
HT	=	*Hevajra Tantra* (ed. Farrow and Memon 1992)
K	=	Kāṇha (my numbering)
P.	=	Pāli
S	=	Saraha (my numbering)
Saṃ	=	R. Saṃkṛtyāyana (1957), *Dohā-koś*
Sch	=	K. Schaeffer (2000), *Tales of the Great Brahmin*
Sh	=	M. Shahidullah (1928), *Chants mystiques de Kāṇha et de Saraha*
Skt.	=	Sanskrit
Sn	=	D. Snellgrove (1954), "Saraha's Treasury of Songs"
ST	=	*Saṃvarodaya Tantra* (ed. Tsuda 1974)
T	=	Tilopa (my numbering)
Tib.	=	Tibetan
Tor	=	F. Torricelli (1997), "The Tanjur Text of Tilopa's Dohākoṣa"

TANTRIC TREASURES

. . . We are not, were not, ever
          wrong. Desire

is the honest work of the body,
          its engine, its wind.
It too must have its sails—wings
          in this tiny mouth, valves
in the human heart, meanings like sailboats
          setting out

over the mind. Passion is work
          that retrieves us,
lost stitches. It makes a pattern of us,
          it fastens us
to sturdier stuff
          no doubt.

—Jorie Graham, "I Watched a Snake"

. . . Do not waver
Into language. Do not waver in it.

—Seamus Heaney, "Lightenings"

Introduction

A Possible Scenario

A thousand years ago or more, a solitary yogin walks out of the Bengali jungle just after sundown and sits cross-legged under the canopy of a village banyan tree. He is dressed in little more than a loincloth. His beard and mustache are unkempt, and his long, matted hair is tied up in a bun. He carries a mendicant's staff and a double-headed hand drum. His eyes shine in the torchlight. His reputation has preceded him, and an audience quickly gathers at his feet, mostly young village men but some women, too. They've heard that he mocks the elders, teaches a way to live freely in the world, and sometimes will perform a miracle, like turning base metals into gold or flying through the sky. Older men cast suspicious glances from the edge of the crowd. They've heard that he's a dropout from the monastic university, lives near a cremation ground with a low-caste woman, participates in debauched rites, works at a low-class occupation if he works at all, and is out to subvert the social and religious order. The silence of evening is broken by the barking of dogs, the lowing of cattle, and the screeching of birds; the scent and haze of home fires fills the air.

When his audience has settled down, the man starts slowly to beat out a rhythm on his drum, and then he begins to sing. His voice is untrained and his melodies rough, but his lyrics are sharp and aphoristic. In rhyming verses, using words from the common tongue, he celebrates the ecstasy of enlightened awareness and the free-roaming life, while mocking the pretensions of ritualists, scholars, contemplatives, ascetics, and anyone who claims that realization can be found anywhere but within oneself. His words are simple, but his meanings complex and full of paradox. He sings of the sky and stars and sea, of animals and plants, of husbands and wives and kings and commoners, but in ways that seem to point below the surface. He says the mind is pure but that we have to do without it; he suggests we can live sensuously in the world but warns against the traps of pleasure; he damns obsession with religious rites but hints at mystical practices of his own; he rails against experts of every sort but venerates his guru without reserve. When he is finished, he gets up, turns his back to the crowd, and walks back alone into the jungle.

The next morning, the village work resumes as it always does, but now some of the young people, and the old men, too, find that they've got the yogin's songs stuck in their heads, a phrase here, a rhyme there, which they try to puzzle out. At odd moments during the day, and even more so at night, they find their thoughts turning to the jungle, to truths that might be discovered beyond the village clearing, to the sound of that strange troubadour's voice, the rhythm of his drum, the look in his eyes.

Uncertainties about Siddhas and Dohās

Siddhas in General

This is at least one way of imagining the origins of the verses translated here, the three surviving Apabhraṃśa-language collections of rhyming couplets, *dohākoṣa*, literally "treasuries of *dohā*" attributed to three Buddhist tantric masters who probably lived in northern India sometime around 1000 C.E.: Saraha, Kāṇha, and Tilopa. These men, and other extraordinary men and women like them, are known collectively as *mahāsiddhas* (great adepts, or great perfected ones, "siddhas" for short).[1] Through the songs they composed, the instructions they left, and the stories that have been told about them they have deeply influenced the shape of religious and literary culture in a number of Asian countries, especially India, Nepal, and Tibet. In India, even after the virtual disappearance of Buddhism in the thirteenth century, their criticism of the status quo and their celebration of a mystical ecstasy attainable through the human body and the grace of a guru helped to set the tone for a variety of later religious movements, including the *sant* tradition of Kabīr and Nānak, certain strains of *bhakti* devotionalism, and aspects of Sufi Islamic mysticism; while in literature they helped to hasten the eclipse of Sanskrit and the rise of various north Indian vernacular languages, whose poetic traditions still carry echoes of their rhymes, rhythm, and imagery. In Nepal, they served as models, and sometimes as deities, for the Buddhist *vajrācaryas* ("tantra experts") among the Newars of the Kathmandu valley, who to this day perform rituals and sing songs that tradition traces to them. In Tibet (and culturally related areas such as Mongolia, Ladakh, Sikkim, and Bhutan), they were seen as charismatic, powerful, wise, and compassionate exemplars of the tantric Buddhist approach to life and as the crucial sources for many important lineages of spiritual practice; at the same time, their songs became models for genres of oral and written poetry that have been immensely popular and influential, whether produced by great hermit yogins like Milarepa (Mi la ras pa, 1040–1123) or powerful clerics like the First Panchen Lama, Lozang Chokyi Gyeltsen (Blo bzang chos kyi rgyal myshan, 1567–1662).

Despite their importance and influence, the siddhas in general, and the three that concern me here in particular, remain profoundly elusive, especially to the historian. We don't know exactly who they were, what religious allegiance they claimed, where or when—or even if—they lived, or how many of the works attributed to them really are theirs.

The most widely disseminated tradition, reflected in a twelfth-century hagiographic collection by the Indian scholar Abhayadattaśrī, tells of eighty-four great siddhas, most of them adepts of the esoteric and controversial Yoginī tantras, an interrelated set of sexually and soteriologically charged texts that flourished among north Indian Buddhists starting around the eighth century, and would become especially important in the "later" (post-1000) orders of Tibetan Buddhism: the Kagyu (bKa' brgyud), Sakya (Sa skya), and Gelug (dGe lugs).[2] Saraha, Kāṇha, and Tilopa all are counted among the eighty-four, as are such equally famous figures as Śavaripa, Virūpa, and Nāropa, and a Nāgārjuna who may or may not be the same as the great Mādhyamika philosopher. There are, however, other treatments of siddhas, with different enumerations and often with different names, such as a partly differing list of eighty-five attributed to Abhayadatta's contemporary Abhayākaragupta; a thirteenth-century Nepalese guru lineage text that mentions nearly two dozen; an eighteenth-century Tibetan account of lineages that relates the stories of fifty-nine—as well as texts that count as siddhas various Indian yoginīs (some of whom appear on other lists, some of whom do not) or the Indian progenitors of the great perfection (*rdzogs chen*) practice tradition popular in the Nyingma (rNying ma) tradition of Tibetan Buddhism (e.g., Mañjuśrīmitra, Garab Dorje [dGa' rab rdo rje], Śrī Siṃha, Vimalamitra, and above all Padmasambhava).[3]

The figures found in these lists are generally acknowledged to be "Buddhists." Certainly, the legends surrounding them and the words attributed to them have influenced countless Buddhists in India, Nepal, and Tibet for a thousand years; but in their original setting, it is not always easy to separate them out—whether in terms of terminology, rhetoric, or practice—from similar figures in non-Buddhist, especially "Hindu" traditions. They seem quite closely related to Śaivite ascetics like the Paśupatas and Kāpālikas; tāntrikas like the Kashmiri Śaivas and Bengali Śaktas; or the wonder-working Nāth siddhas and Rasa siddhas. More broadly, there are general similarities between ideas and practices found in Buddhist siddha writings and those of other Indian yogic and ascetic communities—from such "textualized" movements as those reflected in the *Yoga Sūtra* of Patañjali and the Saṃnyāsa Upaniṣads to such seemingly timeless and "unwritten" groups as the Nāgas, Kaṇphaṭas, and Aghoras.[4] Nor can their possible connections with similar sorts of groups in, for instance, Persia, central Asia, or China be overlooked; the resonance, and possible historical connections, between Indian siddhas and Chinese Chan masters or Taoist immortals suggest an especially intriguing, if uncertain, path for further research. What is more, it is entirely possible that, as suggested long ago by Agehanada Bharati, most of the siddhas actually were pre- or nonsectarian wandering yogins, who appropriated various religious terms without intending to promote a particular religion—yet willy-nilly were appropriated by those very sectarian traditions that they resisted or ignored.[5]

The figures mentioned in the siddha lists often are related explicitly to one another, for instance as guru and disciple, and often are situated in a specific place and/or during the reign of a particular king—many of them, for instance, in north or northeast India during the Pāla and Sena dynasties (c. 750–1250 C.E.). Unfortunately, however, the minimal historical information supplied in one account often contradicts claims made in other sources, or simply is too vague to be interpreted clearly, so that it is very hard to specify that siddha X lived in such and such a place and time and was the disciple of siddha Y and the teacher of siddha Z. Indeed, such discussion begs the question whether many of the siddhas may not simply be literary inventions, no more reliably "historical" than stock characters in epics and folktales the world around. The hagiographies of the siddhas show unmistakable links to Indian narrative traditions dealing with wizards (*vidyādhara*), zombies (*veṭala*), and ghosts (*bhūta*), epic and folk treatments of powerful, capricious *ṛṣis*, and Mahāyāna sūtra celebrations of the heroic bodhisattva. They also beg comparison with the traditions surrounding such universal figures as the saint, the trickster, and the superhero. These mitigating factors—which frustrate so many efforts to understand the religious and cultural history of pre-Muslim India—make it very unlikely that we ever will be able to discover the "historical siddhas."

Hundreds of works of literature are attributed to the siddhas revered in Buddhist traditions; sometimes they have been preserved in Indic languages (usually Sanskrit or Apabhraṃśa), but more commonly they are found in their Tibetan versions, either in the *Tangyur* (*Bstan 'gyur*) collection of "new school" (post-1000) translations or the *Nyingma Gyubum* (*Rnying ma rgyud 'bum*), with its "old school" (pre-850) translations.[6] The siddhas are credited with a tremendous range of types of texts, including initiation ceremonies, maṇḍala rituals, fire offerings, hymns of praise, meditation textbooks (*sādhanas*), and tantric treatises and commentaries, as well as works that deal with such originally nontantric philosophical topics as meditation theory, and Madhyamaka and

Yogācāra ontology and epistemology, not to mention various worldly sciences. The texts that have drawn the most attention, in part because they are the most "personalized," in part because of their impressive literary qualities, are the collections of song-poems in such genres as the dohā (aphoristic couplet), *caryāgīti* (performance song), and *vajragīti* (diamond song). Unfortunately, there is very little way of knowing whether a particular text attributed to a particular siddha—even if that siddha was a historical figure—actually was written by that siddha, so the notion of a "corpus" of texts unambiguously belonging to a specific figure must be regarded with considerable suspicion. This may be even more true in the case of song-poems, where the "texts" most likely were originally oral and were only written down and redacted into collections years, or even centuries, after their composition.

Saraha, Kāṇha, and Tilopa

All of the problems besetting the study of the siddhas in general apply to our attempts to understand Saraha, Kāṇha, and Tilopa. We have multiple, and often utterly conflicting, accounts of their lives and great uncertainties about their relation to the written works attributed to them.

Saraha, the "arrow-maker" disciple of a female tantric practitioner (and also known as the Great Brahmin, or Rāhulabhadra the Younger), is perhaps the greatest single individual in the history of Indian tantric Buddhism, famed as its most eloquent poet; as the fountainhead for lineages of practice related to the Yoginī tantras and to meditation on the "great seal" of reality, mahāmudrā; and as a guru to the immortal Nāgārjuna. Yet we cannot locate him with any precision at all in time or place, probably confound him at times with a disciple called Saraha the Younger, and cannot be certain that two of his most notable poetic works, the "King" and "Queen" Treasuries, were written by him or by a Nepalese master of the eleventh century. Though the *Treasury* translated here is one of the most famous documents of late Indian Buddhism, it exists in multiple, only partly overlapping forms in both Apabhraṃśa and Tibetan. The "standard" Apabhraṃśa version, discovered in a Nepalese royal library in 1907 and published in 1916 by Haraprasād Śāstri, then worked and reworked by Muhammad Shahidullah and Prabodh Chandra Bagchi, never has been found as an independent manuscript but rather has been extracted from a later (eleventh-century?) commentary, in Sanskrit, the *Dohākoṣa-Pañjikā* of Advayavajra—who may be the same as the great Indian tantric theorist Maitripa. In 1929, Bagchi found in Nepal a fragment of still another Apabhraṃśa version that coincides with other editions not at all. Yet another version of the Apabhraṃśa of Saraha's text was discovered by Rahula Saṃkṛtyāyana at Sakya monastery in Tibet in 1934 and published in 1957; it only replicates about half the verses in the "standard" edition. Furthermore, the Tibetan translation contains both common and unique verses, adding further evidence, as if it were needed, of the complexity and fragmentation of the textual tradition surrounding Saraha's signal work.[7]

Kāṇha (also known as Kṛṣṇācārya, the "dark master") is reputed to be an important figure in the transmission lineages of Cakrasaṃvara, a deity whose practice is the focus of a major Yoginī tantra cycle; the author of a brilliant commentary on another Yoginī tantra, the *Hevajra*; a disciple of the great siddha Virūpa; and the skull-bearing (*kāpālika*) composer of a series of controversial performance songs that speak frankly, though also in profoundly symbolic terms, of his relationship with a low-caste woman (*ḍombī*). Yet he, too, is very difficult to locate precisely in time or place, is easily confused with others who bear the common names of Kāṇha or Kṛṣṇa, and may or may not be the author of both the *Treasury* translated here and the performance songs that have earned "Kāṇha" so much notoriety. Kāṇha's *Treasury*, like Saraha's, is not attested by an independent Apabhraṃśa manuscript but rather has been extracted from a later Sanskrit commentary, an anonymous work known as the *Dohākoṣa-Mekhalā-Ṭīkā*.[8]

Tilopa, the "sesame-pounder" (also known as Tillipa, Telopa, or Tailopa), is believed to have received four great tantric teaching streams. Some of the teachings stemmed originally from Saraha, and some of them were transmitted to Tilopa by actual or visionary female figures. He is said to have distilled those into twelve profound instructions that were transmitted, amid great trials, to his disciple Nāropa, who in turn taught his own "six topics" (Tib. *chos drug*) to the Tibetan translator Marpa (1012–1097).[9] From Marpa the teachings passed to Milarepa (1040–1123), thence to Gampopa (Sgam po pa, 1079–1153), from whom nearly all later Kagyu lineages descend. Thus Tilopa is regarded by the Kagyu traditions of Tibet as the direct human source of many of their important practice lineages, including those connected with the tantras they considered the most advanced and effective of all, the Unsurpassed Yoga tantras (Tib. *bla med rnal 'byor rgyud*, Skt. *yoganiruttara or yogānuttara tantras*) and with the radical meditative techniques of the great seal (Tib. *phya rgya chen po*, Skt. *mahāmudrā*). Yet Tilopa, too, is a mysterious character who, just as we think we may approach, melts, like so many other siddhas, into the thicket of historical and textual ambiguity, where doubts remain about his dating, his authorship, and even his historicity. His *Treasury*, too, is unattested as an independent Apabhraṃśa text and also has been extracted from a later Sanskrit commentary, the anonymous *Dohākoṣa-Pañjikā-Sārārtha-Pañjikā*.[10]

What We Do Know

This raft of uncertainties notwithstanding, there are some things we can assert with modest confidence about these three Treasuries and the men who are said to have composed them.

Language and Form

After some initial uncertainties, the language of the *Dohākoṣas* has been identified as an eastern dialect of Apabhraṃśa (sometimes called Avahaṭṭha), which seems to have been employed in Bihar and Bengal for several centuries before, and just after, the turn of the first millennium C.E. Apabhraṃśas—and they are plural, having earlier and later as well as western and eastern versions—were a group of Middle Indo-Aryan languages used in north India from approximately 300 to 1200 C.E. In the sequence of Indian languages, Apabhraṃśas generally fall after the Prākrits (e.g., Pāli, Māgadhī, and Śaurasenī)—which were themselves modifications of classical Sanskrit—and before the rise of the modern north Indian vernaculars, of which the later Apabhraṃśas are the immediate ancestors. The Apabhraṃśas were influenced both by popular speech and the late classical forms of Sanskrit, which, like Latin in the West, persisted as an elite literary language long after it ceased to be widely spoken. The late eastern Apabhraṃśa in which the Treasuries have been transmitted is related most closely to modern Bengali, though its echoes are evident in Assamese, Oriya, Mathili, Bihari, and certain forms of Hindi, too. It is important to note that while eastern Apabhraṃśa prefigures modern north Indian vernaculars in significant ways, and may have been related to the vernaculars of its time, it is—like all Apabhraṃśas—not a vernacular per se but a literary language. Thus, while eastern Apabhraṃśa is the language of the Treasuries, it probably is not the language of the original dohās, close as it may be.[11]

The particular poetic form that is most common in these texts is the dohā, which may refer, depending on context, to a meter or to a type of rhyming couplet dominated by that meter. The dohā gained great importance in the vernacular languages and religious traditions of late medieval north India (where it sometimes was called a *sākhī*), but its earliest exemplifications are found in the collections translated here, and it may derive from still earlier Sanskrit forms, such as the *dodhaka*. As a meter, the dohā is typified by, among other things, a strong end rhyme, a caesura midline, subdivision into smaller rhythmic units, and a close correlation between rhythm and meaning. Perhaps because of its rhythm and rhyme, the dohā frequently has been used as the vehicle for self-contained aphorisms, and above all spiritual advice, whether by the likes of Saraha, Kāṇha, and Tilopa or later figures such as Kabīr, Nānak, or Dādū; it sometimes contains an authorial interpolation, a *baṇa* line, such as "Saraha says."[12] In this sense, the dohā is both a form and genre. As a form, it is also found in two other poetic styles attested in Apabhraṃśa literature, performance songs (*caryāgīti*) and diamond songs (*vajragīti*), which differ generically from dohās because of their different context and function: in performance songs, the couplets are linked together to form a larger unit of meaning, which we might reasonably compare to a Western "song" sung by a singer for an audience (though they might, too, be sung in ritual settings); diamond songs are "songs" in the same sense but differ from performance songs in their purpose: they cannot be understood except within the context of a tantric ritual feast, a "family circle" (*gaṇacakra*).[13]

If a dohā is a self-contained, often aphoristic, rhyming couplet, quite probably oral in its initial transmission, then the very idea of a collection or "treasury" of dohās (a dohākoṣa) is fraught with difficulties. Even if we did not possess multiple and partially incompatible versions of the Treasuries of Saraha, Kāṇha, and Tilopa—which (especially in the case of Saraha) we do—we might reasonably imagine that a text claiming to represent the "authorial intention" of a dohā singer was no such thing, for it is almost certain that various dohās (or groups of dohās; some clearly are related to each other) were uttered in various interactive and public settings, perhaps as the capstone to a religious discourse. Thus it is extremely unlikely that any of the Treasuries translated here—or other collections that are found only in Tibetan translation—actually has been redacted as it was performed.[14] Indeed, we only can assert with confidence that when we examine the *Treasury* of Saraha, Kāṇha, or Tilopa, what we have before us is a later compilation by an editor who, for purposes of his own, brought together dohās or groups of dohās that had come to be associated with one or another of those names, names that might or might not once have denoted an actual person. In this sense, there is probably a considerable amount of arbitrariness built in to the compilation of any single *Treasury*, and though commentators on the texts find order and meaning in their arrangement (sometimes, in fact, it is they who have arranged them!), it is quite imaginable that the texts could have been ordered in many different ways and still been found meaningful by readers.

Content: The Yoginī Tantras as Background

In terms of content, the most historically significant feature of the three dohākoṣas is that each presents clear evidence that its author was familiar with, and probably a practitioner of, the Yoginī tantras. These tantras, which include the *Hevajra, Saṃvarodaya, Caṇḍamahāroṣaṇa, Mahāmudrāṭīlaka, Vajrakīlaya, Catuḥpīṭha, Buddhakapāla*, and *Kālacakra* tantras and texts related to them, are one of the very last literary developments in Indian Buddhism, probably appearing no earlier than the eighth century and gaining importance only in the ninth and tenth centuries.[15] They are related to, but distinguishable from, other late Indian Buddhist tantric textual traditions, including those of the *Guhyasamāja, Yamāri*, and *Vajrapāṇi* tantras, which frequently were designated Mahāyoga tantras. Taxonomists of tantra sometimes assigned the Mahāyoga and Yoginī tantras to separate classes and sometimes placed them together in a single, "highest" class of tantra, the Unsurpassed Yoga tantra.[16] The Yoginī and other "higher" tantras are part of the broader class of Buddhist tantric texts, which began to appear in about the seventh century. All tantras purport to have been spoken by the Buddha in one or another form (most often the form for which the tantra is named), and tantras—along with their voluminous subsidiary literature—quickly began to form an important subset of the Mahāyāna Buddhist canon. By the end of the first millennium, tantra[17] increasingly had come to dominate Indian Buddhist life and practice and, for that matter, to affect life and practice in nearly all Indian religious communities.

Thus, when Buddhism began to make significant inroads in Tibet in the eighth century, tantra already was an inescapable part of Indian Buddhism, and Tibetans regarded the Adamantine Vehicle of tantric practice, the Vajrayāna, as the most advanced of all the Buddha's teachings. All Tibetan Buddhists consider the Yoginī tantras to be at or near the pinnacle of the tantric path. The "old" translation school, the Nyingma, focuses primarily on tantras translated into Tibetan before the Yoginī tantras first arrived in Tibet in the tenth and eleventh centuries, but when it does incorporate aspects of the Yoginī tantras into its characteristic nine-vehicle taxonomy of Buddhist texts and practices, it generally places them in the penultimate category, Anuyoga—beyond the practices of the Disciple and Solitary Buddha paths, standard Mahāyāna, and various lower tantras but still below the apogee of the scheme, Atiyoga, whose texts and practices are the basis of the quintessential Nyingma system, the great perfection. While secondary in the Nyingma, the Yoginī tantras and their commentarial traditions are crucial to the tantric systems of latter-day (post-1000) Tibetan translation schools like the Kagyu, Sakya, and Gelug. Of Yoginī tantra texts and practices, the Kagyu tends to emphasize those related to Cakrasaṃvara (including the female Buddha Vajrayoginī), the Sakya focuses above all on Hevajra, and the Gelug concentrates on Cakrasaṃvara and Kālacakra. Whatever their preferences, all three traditions classify the Yoginī (or "Mother") tantras—along with such "Father" (i.e., Mahāyoga) tantras as the *Guhyasa-*

māja—among the Unsurpassed Yoga tantras that are the highest of the four sets of tantras recognized in their taxonomies (the others being Action, Performance, and Yoga tantras).[18]

Whatever their classification, and despite considerable differences among them with respect to both the outlines and details of theory and practice, the Yoginī tantras are characterized by a number of distinctive features, some of which are unique to them but many of which they share with other highly advanced tantras; with "lower" tantras; with Mahāyāna sūtras, commentaries, and treatises; with Buddhism in general; and with non-Buddhist Indian yogic traditions, including certain schools of Hindu tantra.

The Yoginī tantras have a number of ideas that are distinctive to them:

1. In practices related to reenvisioning the cosmos as a sacred realm, or maṇḍala, an important—and sometimes central—place is given to wrathful, naked, cremation ground–inhabiting female deities, most often called *yoginīs* or *ḍākinīs*. These figures are associated both with profound gnostic wisdom and extraordinary bliss—and the fusion of the two in reality, the mind, and tantric practice. The importance of these figures and their symbolism helps to explain why the Yoginī tantras are named as they are, and also are known as Ḍākinī tantras or Prajñā (i.e., wisdom) tantras.

2. In advanced yogas within the "subtle body" made of channels, winds, and drops, a number of different "seals" (*mudrā*) are identified that help to confirm and deepen one's practice. There are various listings of seals relating to various phases of practice; the most significant set, perhaps, refers to three major procedures: sexual yoga with a flesh-and-blood partner (*karmamudrā*), engagement with a visualized partner (*jñānamudrā*), and nondual contemplation of the nature of reality (the great seal, or *mahāmudrā*). In some Yoginī tantra systems, all are required, while in others only some or one may be applied.

3. A major function of subtle body yogas is to induce a sequence of up to four ecstasies (*ānanda*), which are linked to a variety of other fourfold patterns, for example, four tantric initiations, four moments on the path, four Buddha bodies, and so on. These ecstasies culminate in an enlightened awareness or gnosis—often referred to as "the innate" (*sahaja*) or the great seal (mahāmudrā)—in which the mind's natural purity and luminosity, its nondual realization of emptiness, and an experience of great bliss or ecstasy are indissolubly interfused.

The Yoginī tantras share a number of ideas with other highly advanced tantras:

1. Enlightenment only is possible through confronting and transforming such basic human emotions and events as passion, anger, death, and rebirth, and one must begin to do so during four highly demanding, profoundly sym-

bolic, and in some cases sexually charged initiations received from one's guru, to whom one pledges absolute obedience.

2. The locus for real spiritual work is the human body, and more specifically the subtle body (*sukṣma-śarira*) that interpenetrates and is the basis of our coarse physical bodies. This body consists of seventy-two thousand channels (*nāḍī*), five to ten major breath-related energies (*prāṇa*), and a number of hormonal "drops" (*bindu*) inherited at conception from one's parents.

3. The work of transformation requires overcoming dualistic aversion to notions of pure and impure, a willingness on occasion to transgress conventional moral norms, and skillful manipulation of one's mind and energies so as to bring them to a standstill within certain nodes or centers (*cakra*) within the central channel of the subtle body. In order to harness one's energies, one must be willing on occasion to ingest "impure" substances such as alcohol, semen, and blood, and engage in sexual yoga practices, sometimes within the context of a tantric feast or "family circle," a gaṇacakra. The result of controlling one's energies is the production—or revelation—within the central channel of a blissful, enlightened gnosis.

The Yoginī tantras have certain ideas in common with other Buddhist tantras:

1. One must practice here and now as if one were the Buddha-deity one someday will become, "making the goal the path" by reconstituting oneself out of one's fundamental emptiness as a sacred syllable, which becomes an enlightened being at the center of one's divine, deity-filled abode, the maṇḍala. Through this procedure, one lays the basis for overcoming the three "existential events" at the heart of saṃsāra—death, intermediate existence, and rebirth—and for achieving the dharma, enjoyment, and transformation "bodies" (*dharmakāya, saṃbhogakāya*, and *nirmāṇakāya*) of a Buddha.

2. One must employ a wide variety of ritual and meditative methods, including mantras, supplication prayers, material and immaterial offerings, and the practice of the extraordinary degree of one-pointed concentration required for seeing oneself and the cosmos in an entirely different way.

3. Tantric practice only is possible after initiation and instruction from a qualified guru, who is the key to one's access to tantric Buddha-deities, and to the lineage of gurus who have taught the practices that lead to persons' actually becoming those Buddha-deities.

The Yoginī tantras have a number of ideas in common with a broad range of Mahāyāna Buddhist movements:

1. The purpose of human (and all sentient) existence is to attain fully enlightened Buddhahood—consisting of dharma, enjoyment, and emanation bodies—at the culmination of the path of the "enlightenment hero," the

bodhisattva, who sets out on an arduous spiritual journey motivated by compassion for the sufferings of all sentient beings, and the aspiration to free them all (*bodhicitta*).

2. In progressing toward enlightenment, one must employ a wide range of religious methods (*upāya*) for developing compassion toward all living beings, assisting beings with their worldly and spiritual problems, pleasing a multitude of powerful Buddhas and bodhisattvas, and cultivating one's own visionary experiences of those beings within their Buddha fields, or "pure lands."

3. One must cultivate an approach to wisdom that emphasizes that the nature of all entities and concepts is nonduality, sameness, or, above all, emptiness (*śūnyatā*). This crucial term may variously (and sometimes simultaneously) be understood to mean that things simply lack any substantial, permanent, independent nature (as taught in the Madhyamaka school); that perceived phenomena cannot be differentiated from the mind that perceives them (as taught in the Yogācāra school); and/or that the naturally stainless and radiant mind behind all things is devoid of any of the defilements that appear to blemish it (as taught in literature on the Tathāgatagarbha, or "Buddha nature").

The Yoginī tantras share a number of ideas with Buddhist traditions in general:

1. The essential human problem is repeated rebirth (*saṃsāra*), which is prompted by ignorance of the nature of things, a selfish craving for pleasure, and unskillful actions bearing inevitable effects (*karma*)—but which is capable of elimination (in a condition of peace, knowledge, and bliss called *nirvāṇa*) through proper conduct, the mastery of techniques of meditation, and direct insight into reality.

2. Those who seek spiritual freedom must begin by going for refuge to the Buddha, the doctrine he taught (*dharma*), and the spiritual community he founded (*saṅgha*). Buddhist life usually involves both active participation in a community of like-minded seekers and avoidance of the religious ideas and practices followed by outsiders to the community.

3. It is axiomatic that, in the opening words of the universally revered verse collection the *Dhammapada*, "all that we are is a result of what we have thought: it is founded on our thoughts, it is made up of our thoughts." The implication of this is that as we see, so shall we be.

Finally, the Yoginī tantras share a number of perspectives with non-Buddhist Indian yogic traditions:

1. The saṃsāra-nirvāṇa cosmology is an accurate picture of the lot of all beings everywhere in the universe.

2. Through a combination of personal discipline, virtuous conduct, proper

meditation, and correct insight one may transcend the vicious circle of saṃsāra and attain the transcendent, gnostic bliss of nirvāṇa (or, in Hindu terms, *mokṣa*).

3. The best context in which to pursue spiritual liberation is a supportive community, ideally one built around an experienced and skillful guru.

More specifically, and quite importantly, the Yoginī tantras share with a number of more or less contemporaneous Hindu tantric traditions, whether Kashmiri or Bengali, a considerable number of technical terms, deities, yogic procedures, and social perspectives, to the point where it sometimes is quite difficult to know who has influenced whom, or, as suggested earlier, who belongs to which tradition.[19]

Summary

What all this, then, allows us to assert generally of the Treasuries and their authors is the following. Given their eastern Apabhraṃśa language, the dohās of Saraha, Kāṅha, and Tilopa probably were composed around the end of the first millennium C.E. in northeast India, while the "Treasuries" of dohās that have come down to us are probably somewhat later, and of less certain provenance. Given the dohās' frequent references to matters germane to Mahāyāna Buddhism in general and the Yoginī tantras in particular, their authors are more likely to have been members of a tantric Buddhist comminuty than any other. Knowing that these three dohā composers were familar with, and probably practiced, the Yoginī tantras, we may accept as poetically apt, if not historically demonstrable, the traditional stories that associate them with rejection of conventional social norms, and with resort to forbidden places and practices, including association with female companions. It is at least conceivable that there was a siddha (let us call him Saraha) who learned tantra from a an arrow-making yoginī, that there was another siddha (call him Kāṇha) who kept a low-caste mistress, and that there was still another siddha (call him Tilopa) who received visionary instructions from a ḍākinī. We also may deduce that our authors' seemingly syncretic view of the world—incorporating elements of various tantras, Mahāyāna Buddhism, basic Buddhism, and even Hinduism—simply reflects the creative blend of ideas and practices that make up the weave of the Yoginī tantras. Indeed, it was that creative blend, and their poetic and aphoristic manner of expressing it, that permitted Saraha, Kāṅha, and Tilopa (and other siddhas) to popularize the Yoginī tantras in India (where their echoes still are heard), and their successors to pass them on to Buddhists in Nepal and Tibet, who remember the siddhas to this day as the great progenitors of their traditions of spiritual practice—to the point where their status as flesh-and-blood humans or mythological constructs hardly matters. Besides, *somebody* wrote the dohās, and it's as probable that those somebodies were real individuals named Saraha, Kāṅha, and Tilopa as that they were not.

Common Themes

I hope that the dohās translated here will to some degree speak for themselves, but our appreciation and understanding may be enhanced if I touch at least briefly on six important themes that run through all three collections: (1) a rhetoric of paradox, (2) cultural critique, (3) focus on the innate, (4) affirmation of the body, the senses, and sexuality, (5) promotion of certain yogic techniques, and (6) celebration of the guru.[20]

A Rhetoric of Paradox

Saraha claims that he is declaring everything plainly and holding nothing in secret (S92–93)—yet, like so many texts that belong to what we might call "Asian wisdom literature" (including many Upaniṣads, the Buddhist Perfection of Wisdom sūtras, the classics of "philosophical" Taoism, and the great textbooks of Chan Buddhism), the Treasuries of Saraha, Kāṇha, and Tilopa are difficult to understand without a prior recognition of the rhetoric of paradox that their authors often employ. The hallmark of this rhetoric is the simultaneous or successive assertion of two facts that appear to be mutually contradictory, as in the Keṇa Upaniṣad's claim (2.3), regarding brahman, that "it is conceived of by whom it is not conceived of. . . . It is understood by those who . . . understand it not," the *Heart Sūtra*'s famous affirmation that "form is emptiness, emptiness is form," the *Tao Te-ching*'s insistence (chap. 4) that the "Tao is empty . . . but its capacity is never exhausted," or the Chan *Gateless Gate*'s statement at one time that "mind is Buddha" and at another that "there is no mind, there is no Buddha."[21] Such statements are juxtaposed in part in an attempt to force the reader or listener to push beyond the limits of conceptual thought, which is a bugaboo for almost all the traditions involved. There is more, though: one must understand that apparently contradictory statements often are asserted on two different levels of discourse, what Buddhists usually refer to as the "conventional" and "ultimate." What is true of conventional reality may not be so from an ultimate standpoint, and vice versa, yet each has its particular claim to being "true." Thus, to say that brahman is understood by those who understand it not is not simply to indulge in absurdity: it is to assert that "real" or "ultimate" understanding of brahman only is possible for those who go beyond conventional, conceptual understandings of it; to maintain the identity of form and emptiness is to stress the inseparability, and mutual dependence, of apparently polar ideas; to claim that the empty Tao has inexhaustible capacity is to underline the fact that that which has no fixed nature of its own may become anything at all; while the successive insistence that mind is and is not Buddha shows that, from a certain perspective, the mind is the basis of our enlightenment but from another, even the mind, even Buddha, has no substantial existence, and the recognition of this fact will allow the mind to *become* Buddha. These cursory glosses by no means fully explain the paradoxes that have been offered—it is not that simple—but they do, I hope, demonstrate that interpretation *is* possible.

As heirs to the discursive style of Mahāyāna Buddhism (and perhaps Upaniṣadic Hinduism as well), Saraha, Kāṇha, and Tilopa frequently express themselves paradoxically, either within a single dohā or between one dohā and another, and the key to understanding at least some of what they mean is to be found precisely by recourse to an analysis in which "levels of truth" are parsed. Thus, when Saraha asserts of "the real" (or "that") that "there is no seeing / that doesn't perceive it—/ but it's witnessed solely / at the precious guru's feet" (S17), he may be trying to prod our minds beyond conceptual categories, but he also means to say that although ultimate reality is visible everywhere, the truth evident in every moment and situation, we do not *really* see things that way unless we are instructed on how to do so by a qualified spiritual master. When he says that "your innate nature / neither exists nor doesn't" (S20), he certainly is indicating the inability of conventional thought to capture the ultimate, but he also is pointing out that, from the perspective of one who sees things as they are, one cannot say that the innate (or anything else) has true, substantial existence, while to assert that conventionally we do not possess such an innate, pure nature is to misunderstand our real spiritual potential. When Kāṇha instructs us to "go outside, look around, / enter the empty / and the nonempty" (K11), he certainly is presenting an absurd image of "going outside" to find emptiness and nonemptiness yet can be read, too, as suggesting that we must thoroughly explore the world around us in all its possible permutations if we are to understand it, and ourselves, aright. And when Tilopa asserts that "the precious tree / of nondual mind . . . bears compassion flower and fruit, / though there is no other / or doing good" (T12), he may be suggesting the difficulty of imagining compassion in a mind freed from dualities, but he also is noting that it is precisely *because* of the nondual mind's nondistinction between self and other (or even good and bad) that *true*, nondiscriminating compassion may occur, for compassion that involves discrimination falls short of what compassion can be.

Similarly, in the course of their *collections* of dohās, Saraha, Kāṇha, and Tilopa seem to express contradictory views of many important concepts or practices. Thus, Saraha may instruct his listeners in one place to bow down to mind, which is "the single seed of everything" (S41), and in another to "abandon mind" (S57). Again, it is the *context* in which a term is being used that determines the meaning, and assures coherence: conventional, conceptual mind must be overcome if freedom is to be attained, but the mind that is clear of illusion is the experience of enlightenment, and is in some sense the foundation of all there is, hence a worthy object of worship. Or Saraha may ask in one place "if enjoying things intently / doesn't free you, / . . . how can consciousness be free?" (S19) yet warn in another "don't bind yourself / to sensuous things" (S71). He *may* have some ambivalence about the sensuous world (that would be a typically modern interpretation), but it is likelier that he is insisting, in the spirit of many Mahāyāna and tantric masters, that one must, at one and the same time, *both* involve oneself in the senses *and* maintain detachment from the traps they lay for beings who are in their thrall—that is be in the world but not of it. Or Kāṇha may instruct in one place; "the maṇḍala circle: / knowing how things are, / understand it" (K9), while claiming later: "free from the maṇḍala circle, / I live in / the innate moment" (K18). He appears simultaneously to celebrate and denounce a crucial aspect of the tantric path, the visualization of the maṇḍala, with oneself at the center as a Buddha-deity, yet if the tantric path is admitted to have different stages, for example, the steps of generation and completion, then what is appropriate at an earlier phase (maṇḍala circles) may be largely irrelevant later on. Or, finally, Tilopa may assert in one dohā "I am the cosmos, I am the Buddha, / I am the unadorned" (T16) and then claim in another "I am empty, the cosmos empty, / the triple world empty, too" (T34). The statements appear to be irreconcilable, yet if one understands that from an ultimate point of view emptiness is the nature of all things, then I *am* all there is in terms of their real nature, if not their conventional particulars; alternatively, if all there is is a result or a function of a pure, empty, blissful innate gnosis, and that is what I *am* in the most fundamental sense, then I *am* indeed all things.

These sorts of contradictory statements—now asserting, now denying—are made about many other important ideas, too, ranging from meditation, to emptiness, to nirvāṇa, to tantric practice itself, but in nearly every case the paradox is comprehensible when we think in terms of the different levels of discourse that are being applied in particular contexts. Again, I do not mean to limit interpretation solely to the strategy I have suggested here, for such a strategy is only one among a number that are possible, but I do think that

Saraha, Kāṇha, and Tilopa make more sense in light of such an approach—soundly based in Mahāyāna Buddhist tradition—than they do without it.

Cultural Critique

If there is a type of negation in Saraha, Kāṇha, and Tilopa that seems rather less mitigated by paradox or multiple levels of discourse, it is that related to the three siddhas' attitudes toward social and religious convention, which are aptly summarized by Groucho Marx's famous claim, in *Horse Feathers*, "Whatever it is, I'm against it." In all three collections of dohās, but especially those of Saraha, there hardly is an Indian personage or practice of social or religious importance that is not subjected to mockery or critique. In the first fifteen verses of his *Treasury*, Saraha takes on, in succession, brahmin ritualists (S1–2), who are denounced for their pointless recitations and sacrifices; mendicant ascetics (S3–5), who are mocked for their deceit, hypocrisy, and greed; Jain renouncers (S6–9), who are ridiculed for their obsession with physical austerities; Buddhist monastics (S10), who are chastised for their dress-up games, their intellectualism, and their attempt to desiccate the mind through meditation; Mahāyānists (S11), who are described as sophists and verbal gymnasts; tāntrikas (S11, 14), who are said to be obsessed with mantras, maṇḍalas, and mystic initiations; and practitioners of all kinds (S14–15) who are lampooned for believing that offering lamps or food, going on pilgrimage, or immersing themselves in sacred rivers can purify them of defilement. In other places, Saraha criticizes the self-deception of the alchemists (S51), the absurdities of devoted meditators (S19–20, 22–23, 33, etc.) and the pretensions of scholars (S68, 76, 93) and makes evident his distaste for distinguishing pure and impure on the basis of caste (S46, 56b). Saraha also repeatedly addresses his listener as a "fool" and refers disparagingly to "bestial" or "childish" people who simply don't understand what is right in front of them. In a similar vein, but less extensively, Kāṇha and Tilopa, at various points in their dohās, criticize intellectuals (T8), scholars of sacred literature (K1, 29), people who make offerings to deities and visit pilgrimage spots (T19–21), and tantric ritualists obsessed with "chants, oblations, / and maṇḍala rites" (K29). The social and religious outlook of all three is perhaps best captured in Saraha's injunction: "Throw off / conventional nonsense" (S55).

There are a number of ways in which we might regard these thoroughgoing social and religious critiques, which do not seem to conform with the ecumenical spirit typified by so many Buddhists today. We must recall that, as irenic as it often has been, Buddhism did begin as a movement motivated at least in part by a powerful sense of the inadequacies of the social and religious systems of the mid–first millennium B.C.E., and that satire, caricature, and scorn, along with pointed philosophical criticism, have been part of the Buddhist rhetorical arsenal for a very long time; in this sense, Saraha, Kāṇha, and Tilopa simply are upholding a long-standing Buddhist tradition of pointed inquiry into the ideas and practices of others.[22]

This would help to explain the criticisms of non-Buddhists, and even perhaps of various nontantric Buddhists (for intra-Buddhist polemics have been as vigorous as those directed against "outsiders"), but it does not fully explain the extension of the critique to those who practice the very tradition the siddhas are expounding, the way of the tantras. Here, perhaps, the intent is, in a manner consonant with that of the Mahāyāna Perfection of Wisdom sūtras, to undermine any basis for clinging to any idea or practice that might be taken as valuable in itself, rather than as merely instrumental to true awakening, to root out the complacency that Chögyam Trungpa Rinpoche so aptly labeled "spiritual materialism." Put another way, any concept or technique that is said to lead to freedom through externals of any sort is doomed to failure, for it will have fallen short of touching on the true locus of the perpetuation of saṃsāra or the attainment of nirvāṇa, namely, the innate, nonconceptual, blissful, empty, originally pure mind that is our inmost nature. This innate mind is so internal, so basic, that even meditative practices that seem to point within us are inadequate for its attainment—let alone more obviously outward acts such as offering, chanting, mortifying the flesh, or going on pilgrimage.

In the final analysis, anything that leads to the experience of the innate may be celebrated, even if it appears to contravene accepted ideas and practices; and anything that hinders one from reaching it must be rejected, even if it is a hallowed idea, a well-trodden religious path, an unquestioned class distinction, or an immemorial social taboo. And, as we might expect, a practice that is conducive to experience of the innate in one context may be deleterious to it in another, so we should not be surprised that Saraha, Kāṇha, and Tilopa may, in fact, have done many of things that they criticize others for doing, including performing rituals, going on pilgrimage, engaging in meditation, and, of course, entering into tantric practice—but if they did these things in order to gain the experience of the innate, or from the standpoint of a nondualistic achievement of the innate, then there is no blame attached to their actions. As earlier, the *context* of critique and affirmation are crucial, and since most people are easily deceived by concepts, external practices, and the weight of tradition, it is understandable that the siddhas criticize these more often than they affirm them.

Focus on the Innate

Whether or not Saraha, Kāṇha, and Tilopa really equivocate in their criticism of social and cultural traditions, there can be little doubt as to the great theme they do affirm in their songs: it is the innate, sahaja. In all three, it is the most common term for the ultimate, appearing a total of thirty-one times, far more often than such well-known designations as nirvāṇa, Buddha, emptiness, or the real. Indeed, the term is common enough in various Apabhraṃśa and Sanskrit Buddhist texts of the late first millennium (though especially in the Yoginī tantras and the songs of the siddhas) that early twentieth-century scholars designated the siddhas and others who sang of it "Sahajiyās" and the movement they were believed to represent the "Sahajayāna." The term *sahaja* has received a variety of translations over the years, including "the Innate," "the Together-born," "the Simultaneously-arisen," "the Spontaneous," "Coemergence," "Connate," "Complementarity-in-Spontaneity," and "Being."[23] In its various usages in Indic languages and in Tibetan, it probably denotes or connotes all of these, and more. In common parlance in modern north Indian languages, it refers to what is easy or natural, what one does spontaneously. In more religious or philosophical settings, it may refer to opposing qualities that emerge together, or are held in conjunction, such as existence and nonexistence, or the realization of emptiness and the experience of great bliss. And, in its most technical sense, it designates the most sublime of (usually) four "ecstasies" (Skt. *ānanda*) attained through the practice of the Yoginī tantras, that in which one's inmost nature is revealed, and enlightenment approached or attained. I translate *sahaja* as "the innate" because I think that this captures best the sense it seems to have for Saraha, Kāṇha, and Tilopa, namely, of what is most natural to us, what is most fundamentally our own, what is at the root of our experience of the world—and perhaps of the world itself.

However general or technical the siddhas' usages of "the innate" may be (and, in a given instance, it may be one or the other, or both), it clearly is a major way of describing simply what is most important and most basic—that is, what is ultimate—for those with spiritual aspirations. It is not, however, the only way of describing the ultimate: Saraha, Kāṇha, and Tilopa appear to use it more or less synonymously with a number of other important terms. These include: "great bliss," "stainless mind," "inmost nature," "the real," "great delight," "tasting the same," "that," "knowledge," "self-awareness," "the great seal," "rapture unceasing," "the yoginī," "the union of wisdom and method," "the real nature of thought," "nondual mind," "emptiness," "nirvāṇa," "awakening," "Buddha," "the Thus Gone," "the thought jewel," "the profound," "the singular," "the bodiless," "the self," "the unadorned," "the utmost power," "the single god," "nonthought," "perfection"—and, of course, "the ultimate." There also is a wide range of metaphors that are applied to it, including the sky, the ocean, a mountain, a cave, an elephant, a jewel, a tree, a lotus, a king, home, a lamp, a seed, and a ripened fruit. Furthermore, a multitude of characteristics are attributed to the innate: it is single, motionless, ever the same, pure, stable, pacified—and beyond both virtue and vice, good and bad, self and other, mind and nonmind, empty and nonempty, existence and nothingness, saṃsāra and nirvāṇa. So many terms, so many images, so many predications for a concept reputed to be ineffable! For, as Tilopa remarks, "the real / can't be shown / by the guru's words" (T9a), and the others echo him in various ways, referring to the innate or its synonyms as "something that can't be described" (S52), "without syllable" (S58), "hard to approach" (K15), and most decidedly *not* "what falls within the range of thought" (T9).

Keeping this caveat in mind, we still may make a number of conventional observations about the ways in which Saraha, Kāṇha, and Tilopa think of the innate and its cognates. The first is that, in line with longstanding Indian ways of conceiving the ultimate, it is described both negatively and positively. While Buddhism has a reputation for characterizing reality primarily in negative terms (e.g., as nonself, or emptiness), in fact, from the earliest scriptures on, it has provided many positive terms for the ultimate, too, from specifications in the Pāli *nikāyas* that nirvāṇa is not just extinction but also in some sense involves knowledge and bliss; to claims in Mahāyāna that the mind, whether in potential form as Buddha nature (the matrix of the Thus Gone: Skt. *tathāgatagarbha*) or in fruition as the Buddha's dharma body (*dharmakāya*), is, though empty by nature, nevertheless replete with all possible virtues; to descriptions in tantric texts of both the nature of reality and the outcome of the path as the adamantine (*vajra*) body, speech, and mind, or the gnosis in which realization of emptiness and experience of great bliss are inseparable. Buddhists will disagree among themselves as to how literally this or that characterization of the real is to be interpreted, and it is worth underscoring the fact that for every thinker who sees emptiness as a simple negation of any metaphysical self or substance anywhere, there usually will be another who understands it as negating self or substance in *worldly* entities, while at the same time implying the enlightened mind's ultimate emptiness of any delusion or stain (i.e., anything *other* than it) and its maximal possession of all possible virtues. I would not claim with certainty that either of these perspectives—which in Tibet were termed the "intrinsic emptiness" (*rang stong*) and "extrinsic emptiness" (*gzhan stong*) views—is necessarily that of Saraha, Kāṇha, and Tilopa, but there is little doubt that tantric literature in general is very amenable to the "extrinsic emptiness" approach, while still being interpretable from the "intrinsic emptiness" standpoint.[24]

The second observation is that the innate seems to possess characteristics that are both ontological and epistemological. In other words, it is "the real" (Skt. *tattva*), that which is most "objective," true, or fundamental about what there is, but it also involves what, for want of a better term, we might call "experience," a "subjective" apprehension of things that is associated with a variety of terms connoting mentality, including "mind" (Skt. *citta*), "thought" (*manas*), "comprehension" (*buddhi*), and knowledge, or gnosis (*jñāna*). One of its most common descriptions in tantric literature, especially in the traditions of the Yoginī tantras, is as a gnosis in which the realization of emptiness and an experience of great bliss are combined—and it is not just "knowledge" and "feeling" that are combined but the perception and what is perceived, so that the mind that sees emptiness also *is* emptiness, and the bliss that is felt by the subject also is a quality of objects that are apprehended. In a Western philosophical context, this conflation of ontological and epistemological might be seen as a category mistake of the first order; in India, however, at least from the time of the Upaniṣads on, it has been common to predicate of the ultimate (to the degree that one could predicate anything of it) that it is the most of whatever is positive, including reality, knowledge, and happiness, or bliss. Hindus maintained that brahman's nature was reality-knowledge-bliss (*sat-cit-ānanda*), while Buddhists insisted that nirvāṇa and/or Buddhahood involved a "permanence" lacking in worldly events, a supremacy of knowing (perhaps even omniscience), and the greatest possible pleasure. Hence, in an Indian setting (as perhaps in a theological context in the West), it made perfect sense to say that the ultimate was both objective and subjective, ontological and epistemological, for part of what made it ultimate was its transcendence—or combination—of dualities that are irreconcilable on a conventional level.

A third and final observation about the innate is that it seems to be conceived in a manner that is at once psychological and cosmological. Clearly, if it is to be identified with "the mind," at least in its purified condition, it is generally what we might call a "psychological" concept; yet it is not *merely* a psychological notion, for Saraha, Kāṇha, and Tilopa all clearly believe that the mind is not just a subjective capacity that this or that individual possesses, through which the world might be "known," with or without the help of concepts. No, the awakened mind is far greater than that: it is the "single seed of everything" (S41), from which "you'll emit / the whole triple world, / then draw it back again" (K17), where "things rise and . . . set" (S88a), and "all is forever fixed" (S103), and which, though "drained of all color, / lacking a shape," is nevertheless "fulfilled in every appearance" (T32). In short, the mind, hence the innate, seems to function as a cosmological—even cosmogonic—principle, serving as the source and substance of things as surely as it is a capacity for the cognition of things. In this respect, again, the tantric authors of the dohās belong to a well-established tradition in Indian religious thought, wherein there is a close relation between the microcosm of human mental activity and the macrocosm of the creative processes of the cosmos. Whether they claim, as do many Hindus, that our individual psychology is an aspect of an ultimate reality that in some sense is or has "mind," or maintain with various Buddhists that the cosmos is affected or even effected by our thoughts, Indian philosophers repeatedly have recognized the relation between ontogeny and cosmogony, between psychology and cosmology—and Saraha, Kāṇha, and Tilopa appear to accept the relation, too. How "strongly" they intend the relation is another question. Just as there are interpreters of the positive images of the innate in the dohās who will insist that all such imagery must be taken as merely metaphoric (since ultimately, reality *only* can be described negatively, as empty), so will there be interpreters of the dohās' cosmopsychological language who will take it symbolically, as, for instance, merely indicating the *importance* of mind in the world rather than mind's substantive, magical creation of it; or indicating that the mind's identity with the world is merely in terms of the emptiness that is the common nature of all things and minds. As earlier, multiple readings are possible—but also as earlier, the dohās probably lend themselves more naturally to the "literal" reading, even while leaving the figurative readings open, as well.

However we regard the innate—whether we accept its ineffability, try to resolve its complexities, or simply see it as a classic Indian attempt to articulate the ultimate in paradoxical terms—it remains *the* crucial term in the lexicon of Saraha, Kāṇha, and Tilopa, for it is what, if we are to be free, we must attain, realize, experience, become. In a certain sense, of course, everything *is* it, and everything is already awake—yet most of us maintain at least the illusion of error and pain, and until we are rid of that, until we understand who we really are and always have been, we will remain in bondage. Thus, though the innate already is perfected in all of us, we still require methods of one sort or another to help us realize this fact, and recover what never has been lost. The two most important methods prescribed by Saraha, Kāṇha, and Tilopa are (1) an affirmation of the body, the senses, and sexuality, and (2) the promotion of certain yogic techniques—though, as I will show, they do not prescribe either method without noting some important contraindications.

Affirmation of the Body, the Senses, and Sexuality

India is famous for having developed some of the world's most extreme forms of asceticism. As early as the time of the Buddha, and probably before, various wanderers and forest dwellers sought to overcome mortal afflictions by conquering, and ultimately transcending, the body. To do so, they deprived themselves of food, shelter, and clothing, stopped their minds and senses, and in some cases went as far as standing in a single spot for years on end or fasting unto death. We are told in canonical texts that the Buddha, after rejecting the hedonism of royal palace life, pursued such self-mortification with great zeal but in the end rejected that way of life as well, arriving at a "middle way" between the two extremes, which found its expression primarily in the rules of conduct for Buddhist monastic orders. While moderate by ancient Indian standards, however, the rules of Buddhist monastic life, and the attitudes informing them, clearly reflect a considerable suspicion of the body, the senses, and sexuality, all of which are said to feed desire—and desire, or craving, or attachment, was believed by the Buddha to be a primary cause for the continuing rebirth in saṃsāra that he saw as the basic problem of sentient existence.

Such an attitude is predominant in the canonical and postcanonical literature of non-Mahāyāna schools and to this day affects the normative Theravāda outlook that is the "official" Buddhism of Sri Lanka and most of southeast Asia. And although a few Mahāyāna texts suggest that a bodhisattva's compassionate action in the world may require engagement with the body, the senses, and even sexuality, or that a bodhisattva with perfect wisdom will not distinguish between pure and impure, or worldly and transcendent, in most Mahāyāna sources the traditional suspicions remain firmly in place. It is only with the rise of tantric movements in the late first millennium C.E. that a real shift in Buddhist values becomes evident. As I have shown, tantric movements in general believe that the human body is a crucial locus for spiritual work and that the various energies and emotions housed within that body may, if properly reenvisioned or transformed, serve as causes of enlightenment rather than hindrances to it. I also have shown that the more "advanced" tantras, including the Yoginī tantras practiced by many of the siddhas, may incorporate sex, and other types of religiously unconventional behavior, into the Buddhist path. Tantric attitudes and actions are justified by their theorists and practitioners as a logical extension of the nondual outlook and commitment to skillful religious methods that are so much a part of the Mahāyāna—but that only makes them seem slightly less at odds with a puritanical code that held sway in India for so long.

Certainly, Saraha, Kāṇha, and Tilopa are quite explicit in their insistence that the body, the senses, and even, in certain contexts, sexuality are to be embraced rather than shunned by those who seek freedom. One of Saraha's major critiques of the Jains is that they seek to gain freedom by discarding the body (S9), when, in his own experience, "I've seen / no place of pilgrimage / more blissful than the body" (S48). He criticizes the scholar who does not know that "Buddha / dwells within his body" (S68), and instructs, as well, that "what's bodiless / is hidden in the body: / know this, and you're freed there" (S89). Kāṇha, similarly, sings of gaining "awakening / in this body" (K29) and specifies that "natural bliss is seen / . . . in your inmost body" (K3)—probably a reference to the subtle body that is so crucial to success in practicing the Yoginī tantras.

It is not just that the body is to be accepted and understood; the senses that are part of it must be used as well. Saraha instructs his listeners to "look to the senses—/ there's nothing / I'd exclude from them" (S43a); and, addressing one who is "beyond all renouncing," he asks, "if enjoying things intently / doesn't free you, / . . . how can consciousness be free?" (S19). In the same spirit, Kāṇha invites us to "indulge in play" and asks why we should not "entertain / the five senses" (K28), while Tilopa points out that "aggregates, elements, / fields, and the senses—/ all are bound up / in your innate nature" (T1).

Not only may the senses be used and embraced but sexuality itself, often seen as the most destructive manifestation of sense desire, is acceptable, too. Saraha refers casually to "living at home with your wife" (S19); includes among the practices that "perfect the transmundane" "eating and drinking, / enjoying bliss" (S24); devotes a number of verses to celebration of a yoginī who may well be his female companion (S83–87); and asks pointedly (referring to tantric symbols for the vagina and penis): "delighting in / the rapture between / lotus and vajra / . . . who in the triple world / could not have their hopes fulfilled?" (S94). Similarly, Kāṇha asks a "maiden" of his acquaintance, "without your ceaseless passion, / how will I gain awakening?" (K29) and Tilopa instructs his listeners: "don't disparage the physical woman" (T25)—the action seal (karmamudrā) through sexual practices with whom enlightenment may be hastened—and adds that sublime experience is possible in "a passionate woman's embrace" (T27a).[25]

All this might seem to add up to clear proof that the siddhas, as both ancient and modern critics have claimed, are guilty of hedonism and antinomianism, their quest for the innate fueled by indulgence in pleasures that more sober and upstanding Indian spiritual traditions have found to be the path to ruin—an indulgence that they cannot or will not counteract because it is part of their conception of the ultimate that "in it, there is / no vice or virtue at all" (K10). It is not nearly so simple, though, for scattered throughout the Treasuries are enough echoes of traditional Buddhist cautionary rhetoric that we cannot assert that their attitudes toward the body, the senses, and sexuality are entirely unambiguous. Saraha, for instance, speaks of a time when "the body's bonds are broken" (S46), "senses subside" (S29) "desire indeed is destroyed" (S50), or "all appearance / collapses before your eyes" (S74a); and, citing various desire-entranced animals as negative examples, instructs his listeners: "Don't bind yourself / to sensuous things" (S71). He also cautions against indulgence in sex—especially in a tantric context—without proper insight and discipline, asking, "If you don't grasp / everything as it is, / how, in the midst of sex, / will you perfect great bliss?" (S91). Similarly, Tilopa speaks of a point on the path when "senses and their objects / no longer appear" (T5). More broadly, all three siddhas make it clear that ethical distinctions *do* matter, as when they criticize pseudosages who "don't know right / any more than wrong" (S3) or exalt such classic Buddhist virtues as compassion and generosity (S15ab, 107–109, 112; T2, 12).

Are we then to believe that Saraha, Kāṇha, and Tilopa really are just good old-fashioned Buddhists, maintaining traditional suspicions of the body, the senses, and sexuality, promoting an ascetic ideal and a transcendent ultimate? The answer, unsurprisingly, seems to be yes and no. There certainly are enough cautionary indications in their dohās to suggest that the siddhas did not seek to obliterate all ethical distinctions and, furthermore, understood very well that the body, the senses, and sexuality really could lead one astray and needed to be controlled if one was to attain enlightenment. Unlike their more traditional predecessors, however, they did not seek control through rejection or avoidance but rather through active engagement guided by wisdom, skill in various methods, and—crucially—the advice of an experienced guru. Indeed, there are a number of songs where the ideal of being "in the world but not of it" is made fairly explicit, as when Saraha describes a yogin who is "enjoying things, / unstained by things. . . . / untroubled by things, enjoying things" (S64), or another who "seized / by the elephant trunk of senses,/ . . . seems to die, / but . . . / like a skillful trainer, / escapes and goes away" (S101); and when Tilopa instructs his audience: "Like a poison expert / partaking of poison, / delight in existence / but don't get hooked on existence" (T24).

There is, thus, a certain balance that the practitioner must strike. Virtue, discipline, detachment: all are required, and if they seem to be denigrated, that is because, when one adopts the perspective of the ultimate, they do not really exist; conventionally, however, they are a part of what one must practice if one is to experience the ultimate, for as Saraha reminds his listeners, "not comprehending the innate, / you're in the grip of vice" (S63). Once one *has* comprehended the innate, the ultimate, it turns out that it is a condition that itself transcends the classical distinction between turbulent saṃsāric existence and a quiescent nirvāṇa, what is referred to in Mahāyāna as "nonabiding nirvāṇa" (*apratiṣṭhanirvāṇa*): Saraha describes the nondual mind as "free from existence— / and from nirvāṇa" (S110), Kāṇha tells of a state where "delighting in existence, / you'll still perfect nirvāṇa" (K22), and Tilopa urges his listeners to "honor Buddha / by nonconceptual mind; / Hey! Don't get stuck in existence—/ or nirvāṇa" (T22).

In short, the body *is* the locus of spiritual work, and one should not seek freedom anywhere but within it (or the subtle body that is its "inmost" aspect)—yet one should not simply indulge it; the senses *are* to be entertained, for they are no less (or more) real and important than less tangible aspects of the world—yet they cannot be allowed to master one; and sexuality *may* be used in the pursuit of the spiritual, for it is an intensive expression of many of our (and the cosmos's) most fundamental energies—yet one must be sufficiently disciplined in practicing it that it will not lead to a deterioration of compassion or wisdom. And, as I now will show, the way one maintains the balance required for living "naturally" in the world, sensuous and spiritual at the same time, is through certain yogic practices.

Promotion of Certain Yogic Techniques

As is evident from the commentaries written on them, the Treasuries of Saraha, Kāṇha, and Tilopa have been regarded by Buddhist practitioners in India, Nepal, and especially Tibet not just as works of poetic or philosophical genius or incisive social commentary but as systematic guides to practicing the Buddhist path, and in particular to describing and promoting certain yogic techniques that are conducive to enlightenment.[26] Before we concede the truth of this assumption, however, we must acknowledge that in none of the three texts are verses of advice on yogic practice laid out in a completely straightforward manner; rather, they come up here and there, interspersed among other verses with other concerns, which makes it difficult to ascertain what the priorities of the author must have been—especially when we recall that the Treasuries reflect choices most likely made by editors rather than authors, and the connection between a collection of dohās and an individual author is tenuous at best.

Furthermore, all three collections contain what we might regard as "antiyogic" rhetoric, which may leave us further confused as to what the siddhas were promoting and what they were denigrating. There are, for instance, numerous passages in which Saraha warns his listeners that meditation (Skt.

dhyāna) and contemplation (*bhavanā*), which are quintessentially yogic exercises, are actually worthless: "You're deceived by meditation, / so why meditate?" (S22); "mind is unstained—/ don't taint it with meditation" (S23); "meditation: / why look for freedom in a lie?" (S33); "the whole cosmos / is deluded by meditation" (S35). Saraha also questions the value of the breath control that is essential to so many yogic practices, wondering in one place what a yogin who has succeeded in stopping the breath will do when death time comes (S66) and in another instructing a "wretched yogin": "Don't hold your breath / and think on yourself; / . . . don't focus in / on the tip of your nose" (S44). Rather more surprisingly, given my earlier claim that the siddhas were almost certainly practitioners of the Yoginī tantras, there are as well a number of passages that disparage the yogic techniques most associated with tantra, such as repetition of mantras (S14, 23, 39), visualization of the maṇḍala circle of deities (S11, K18, 29), and, as I have shown, sexual yoga (S94).

These passages do pose prima facie problems for an interpreter who wishes to see the Treasuries as guides to meditation or other yogic techniques, but the problems are not insurmountable. We must recall that in any Buddhist wisdom text a negation, whatever the object, may at times be conveyed solely at an ultimate level of discourse, such that, for instance, when Saraha criticizes meditation or maṇḍala practice, he does so in order to "empty" them of any substantial existence we might attribute to them or any attachment we might develop toward them. Such an ultimate level of negation does not mean that, in a conventional sense, one does not meditate or visualize a maṇḍala. Quite the contrary, it most likely is *through* yogic practices of one sort or another that one will *truly* learn how to overcome attachment to entities instinctively taken to be substantially existent. We also must recall that, in the complex sequence that is any individual's Buddhist path, practices that are necessary at one point may be counterproductive at another: there are disciples for whom meditation or maṇḍala practice may be useful at one time but for whom at other times the same practices may turn into dead ends that must be transcended. Many of the dohās collected in the Treasuries may first have been given as a particular piece of advice for a particular audience in a particular context, but we no longer know that context, so we simply juxtapose statements that seem, at times, to contradict each other.

In fact, the preponderance of the evidence from the three Treasuries indicates that Saraha, Kāṇha, and Tilopa all did promote specific yogic practices, which were believed crucial to the listener's ability to attain the ultimate. There are several yogic themes that appear repeatedly, not all of them consistent at first glance, including exhortations to: (1) control, or even stop, the mind and/or breath; (2) relax the mind, or simply see it as it actually is; (3) meditate with the aid of mantras and maṇḍalas; (4) understand the subtle body and its component parts; and (5) induce—perhaps with the aid of sexual yoga—a series of four momentary ecstasies, of which the "innate" is the highest.

Stopping Mind

Saraha advises his audience several times to bring thought and/or breath to a standstill, urging, for instance, "where thought and breath / no longer roam, / and sun and moon don't shine—/ there, fool, repose / your mind!" (S25) and describing a point when "winds enter mind . . . [and] utmost bliss / can't be contained" (S42c). Kāṇha sings in symbols of how "thought / can't possibly escape / when motionless breath, / the mistress, remains at home" (K13). And Tilopa describes as "the self-aware fruit of the real" the place where "mind has died," hence "breath / is completely dissolved" (T7), and asserts that "where mind is becalmed, / the triple world dissolves" (T11a). There are a number of passages, too, in which the mind (or thought) is singled out for denigration and identified as something to be transcended on the path. Saraha sings: "When thought's been changed / to nonthought, / you'll gain thereby / unsurpassed awakening" (S42a) and asserts that "the world / is bound by mind, / and no one at all can grasp / the nonmind" (S78); he also celebrates the yoginī who appears before him "mind destroyed" (S85). Tilopa, similarly, exclaims: "Mind must be killed! / Destroy it with nirvāṇa" (T3), and advises: "Don't disparage unthinking" (T4), since "what falls within / the range of thought / is not the ultimate" (T9).

These passages in which mind is in one way or another negated echo longstanding attitudes in yogic communities, where, as early as the time of the *Yoga Sūtra*, Patañjali could define yoga itself as "stopping the fluctuations of mind" (*citta-vṛtti-nirodha*) and where language and conceptual thought always have been regarded as hindrances to a direct experience of reality as it actually is—however that reality might be defined.[27] More specifically, it is assumed in nearly all yogic systems that mind and breath are intimately related, so control of the one will enhance control of the other. In the specific yoga system of the Yoginī tantras, the experiences of ecstasy and enlightenment that lie at the culmination of the path are impossible without becalming the conceptual mind and the breath, so that one may work with clarity and care in the subtle body.

Relaxing Mind, Seeing Mind

In still other passages, the siddhas seem to suggest that, far from controlling or trying to "kill" mind (and/or breath), one ought simply to let it go, or just see it as it is. Thus, Saraha recommends: "Releasing thought / and breath, / like unsteady horses, / dwell in your innate nature" (S45) and notes that, like a camel, "bound, it runs / in all directions, / freed, it stands there motionless" (S43). He sings of the yoginī, a symbol for enlightened awareness, that "she eats, she drinks, / she doesn't care / what appears" (S86), and also likens the mind to a massive elephant that must be freed, and allowed to "drink the river's water, / and dwell on the shore as it pleases" (S100). In a similar fashion, Tilopa instructs: "Let thought go / where it wishes—/ it can't go wrong there" (T35). There also are a number of important verses in which seeing mind just as it is, as empty and/or pure, is required. Saraha advises us to "grasp the mind / as being like space; / as naturally spacious / grasp the mind to be" (S42a); asserts that "if mind is indicated / by mind, / concepts are held in suspension . . . / [and] mind dissolves / into its nature" (S78b); and instructs: "Witness mind with mind, fool, / and be free / from every base view" (S99). He also urges his listener to "just recognize mind wherever you are / [since] all is unceasingly fixed / in awakening" (S103), and to "bring forth / the stainless nature of mind, / quite beyond concepts" (S104). The mind's innate flawlessness and luminosity is celebrated repeatedly by all three siddhas, from Saraha's assertion that it is "is quite naturally pure" (S106), to Kāṇha's description of it as "beyond defilement" (K10), to Tilopa's claim that it "is stainless, beyond existence and nothingness" (T11).

All of these instructions to release mind, or see it as it is, or let its purity shine seem quite different in spirit from the denigrations of mind and thought I examined in the previous subsection, yet they need not be seen as contradictory if we acknowledge that a word like "mind" or "thought" may be used in more than one way and with more than one sort of valuation. This double usage is nowhere more evident than in Kāṇha's description of nirvāṇa as the place "where thought / has nothing to do / with thinking" (K20) or in Tilopa's advice to "kill the thought / that is not rooted in mind" (T33). Thus, conceptual mind or thought may be an obstacle to enlightenment, but mind or thought released into its essential nature (as pure, empty, blissful, etc.) *is* enlightenment.[28] The latter is a characterization of the goal (though also, at times, a means to the goal) while the former is a concern solely on the path—as long as one recognizes which stage of practice is being described, one need not feel (pardon the expression) any cognitive dissonance.

Using Mantras and Maṇḍalas

There are several passages that make it clear that, whatever their occasional criticisms of reciting mantras or visualizing maṇḍalas, these traditionally tantric practices *are* a part of the siddhas' spiritual repertoire. Saraha sings cryptically of the "single syllable" he knows, though he admits, "friend, / I don't know its name" (S90), and he describes a syllable, amid the "uncorrupted three" (perhaps the purity of body, speech, and mind), that is synonymous with "the god" (S90a). Saraha also discusses the maṇḍala circle, asserting that it is created by Śukra—a multivalent term that refers to the planet Venus but also to the drop of semen whose manipulation within the subtle body is crucial to the attainment of tantric ecstasies (S98). Kāṇha refers in a number of places to the mantric syllables or phrases, including *haṃ* (which is, in fact, associated with Śukra) (K4); *evaṃ*, which, in the Yoginī tantras and other advanced tantric systems, refers to a complex set of polarities, including emptiness and compassion, female and male, and breath and mind (K6, 21); and an unidentified "syllable of truth" at which an accomplished master stops his mind (K23) and where "zenith and nadir / both are unseen" (K24). He also instructs his listeners to understand the maṇḍala circle (K9) and speaks of emitting "the whole triple world" and drawing it back again (K17) and attaining the ultimate "in the company of wrathful goddesses" (K18), presumably those of a Yoginī tantra maṇḍala.

These references do not add up to a clear picture of what sort of mantra and/or maṇḍala practice the siddhas might have performed, but it does indicate that such practice was part of the religious world in which they moved, and may have been a part of what they advised their listeners to practice, too. Certainly, the notion of sound and syllables as creative realities has been part of Indian thought for millennia, and the notion of a yogin's participation in a divine world just as old. They form an important aspect of virtually all tantric practices, including those of the advanced tantras with which Saraha, Kāṇha, and Tilopa were familiar. On the basis of what we know about the practice of the Yoginī tantras from such texts as the *Hevajra Tantra* and *Saṃvarodaya Tantra*, we might speculate that the siddhas would engage in intensive visualization practices, in which they would reduce themselves and the world to emptiness, then reimagine both their world and themselves as divine. First, out of emptiness, they would generate certain Sanskrit "seed" syllables, corresponding to the great elements, which would transform into the basic maṇḍala mansion that would serve to house divine inhabitants. Next, from the emptiness where they themselves had been, they would generate another seed syllable, which in turn became themselves in the form of a male, female, or sexually joined male/female Buddha-deity, surrounded by other deities generated from their own seed syllables, often wrathful goddesses; these were the maṇḍala's inhabitants. Maintaining a vision of themselves as possessing a divine body, uttering mantras as their deity speech, and maintaining as best they could a nondual, blissful mind like that of a Buddha, they would practice emitting and withdrawing from themselves the transformed world of the maṇḍala, along with its deities, perfecting thereby their powers of concentration, and strengthening their recognition of their own ultimate divinity. These practices, complex and important as they are, were in the Yoginī tantras only preliminary to the more subtle and truly transformative practices performed within the subtle body, and it may be because of their preparatory nature that the siddhas seem at times to disparage elements of maṇḍala-centered yogas.

Working Within the Subtle Body

That we possess a subtle body (*sukṣma-śarira*) is, as already noted, a common assumption in many yogic systems and, though never named as such, an implicit context for many instructions in the dohās of Saraha, Kāṇha, and Tilopa. The subtle body is probably the referent when Kāṇha sings of the "inmost body" (K3) and is likened by him to both a lotus (K4–5) and a mountain (K14–15, 25–26). References to "sun and moon" (e.g., S25, 47, K4) or the Ganges and Yamuna rivers (S47) are in a tantric context commonly understood to denote the left and right "outer" channels of the subtle body, and a term like "the in between" (S30) or "the middle" (K24) may easily be interpreted to refer to the central channel, which is where the mind and the breath-related physical energies (prāṇa) that are at the basis of ourselves and the world originate, and to which they must return, if real spiritual work is to be performed. The nodes where the "outer" channels intersect the central channel are called "wheels" (cakras), each of which (there usually are four or five) is a focal point for various substances and attributes, as well as for various meditative practices. Saraha sings of "ever filling the cakras / again and again" (S24), and Kāṇha makes numerous references to the "lotus" that, among other things, connotes the cakras (e.g., K3–7). Within the subtle body, the yogin must manipulate mind, breath, and various drops so as to induce the ultimate awareness that is the goal of completion-stage practices. Therefore, the many references (mentioned earlier) to the "place" where mind and breath are stopped must be understood in most cases to connote the central channel, and in particular either the crown cakra or the heart cakra.

The crown cakra (symbolized by Kāṇha as the summit of a mountain) is asserted in many Yoginī tantras to be the residence of the blissful white semen drop we each inherit from our father, and it is the manipulation, retention, and refinement of this drop—also referred to as the awakening mind (bodhicitta) (K3), the thought jewel (K16, K31), or the utmost gem (T27a)—that is the basis of the ecstatic experiences so important to practitioners of the Yoginī tantras. The heart cakra is mentioned somewhat less frequently in the Treasuries—Saraha does note that "what rises in the heart / settles in the heart" (S73)—but it is an important locus in the context of many advanced tantric practices, where it is in the "indestructible drop" at the heart that the subtlest mentality and materiality, the basis of life, death, and rebirth, is to be found. The subtlest mentality-materiality is therefore our inmost nature, or innate awareness, our "Buddha nature," which must be purified if we are to attain enlightenment. In any case, whatever their specific cakra references, the siddhas do believe that it is only through drawing mind and breath-related energies into the central channel, then to the crown and/or heart cakras, that conceptuality and physical restlessness will be stilled and real progress toward freedom made possible.

Ecstasy and Sexual Yoga

Within the context of the subtle body, the practice of greatest importance to Saraha, Kāṇha, and Tilopa would seem to be the production of a series of four momentary ecstasies of increasing intensity and ultimacy: ecstasy (ānanda), utmost ecstasy (paramānanda), ecstasy of cessation (viramānanda), and innate ecstasy (sahajānanda). Though they do not use the term "ecstasy" in more than a handful of verses (e.g., S96, T25, T27, T28), it is probable that most, if not all, of their many references to "the innate" are a sort of shorthand for "innate ecstasy," which is the fourth and highest in the series, perhaps identical to enlightenment itself.

There are a variety of descriptions of how the ecstasies are induced. They first are encountered in the course of the four initiations—Vase, Secret, Wisdom-Gnosis, and Fourth—that are required for undertaking Yoginī tantra practice.[29] In most accounts of postinitiation yogic practice, the ecstasies presuppose the "dissolution" of conceptual mind and coarse energies within the central channel, followed by the generation of heat energy from the red female drop at the navel cakra, which rises up the central channel and melts the blissful white male semen drop that resides at the crown cakra. In some accounts, then, that drop descends immediately to the navel cakra, where it is held, and ecstasy experienced; when the drop is raised to the heart cakra, utmost ecstasy is experienced; when it reaches the throat cakra, the ecstasy of cessation is experienced; and finally, when it returns to the crown cakra, innate ecstasy—which utterly transcends the other three and is tantamount to enlightenment—is experienced. In other accounts, the four ecstasies are said to proceed in descending and ascending phases. In the descending phase, when the white drop at the crown reaches the throat cakra, ecstasy is attained; when it reaches the heart, utmost ecstasy is attained; when it reaches the navel, ecstasy of cessation is attained; and when it reaches the tip of the sexual organ, innate ecstasy is attained. These ecstasies are "ordinary," but when ecstasy is conjoined with the realization of emptiness, one experiences extraordinary ecstasies: one draws the drop back up the central channel, through ecstasy at the navel, utmost ecstasy at the heart, ecstasy of cessation at the throat, and, finally, innate ecstasy at the crown. In any scenario, the culmination of the process is the attainment of an innate ecstasy that involves the simultaneous experience of bliss and realization of emptiness.[30]

I have noted already that Saraha, Kāṇha, and Tilopa all make references to female partners with whom they appear to have sexual relationships, and it is probably within the context of these subtle body practices that these references should be understood. Again, less from their own dohās than from other Yoginī tantra contexts, we may suggest that the peerless coquettes, passionate maidens, and incomparable yoginīs of whom the siddhas sing were their partners in highly specialized and difficult practices whose primary purpose was to "force" energies into or within the subtle body so that they could be employed there for the purpose of hastening enlightenment. One of the reasons why sexuality may be used yogically is that, more than any other human activity, sexual intercourse, even in an "ordinary" context, has the effect of bringing thought and energy into the central channel, stilling conceptuality, inducing pleasure, and melting the white drop at the crown cakra, which then is "emitted" at the time of orgasm. In general, however, the ecstasies of tantra only are possible if, rather than being emitted, the white drop is retained, and one's bliss combined with a realization of the empty nature of phenomena, which may form the basis of one's transformation into an enlightened Buddha-deity. Thus, tantric sexual practices require immense discipline, great mental and physical self-control. Ironically, though they use "desire" to hasten the achievement of enlightenment, they cannot be practiced successfully by people in whom desire is uncontrolled and reality misunderstood. This, no doubt, is one of the reasons why Saraha cautions those who, failing to grasp things as they are, think that "in the midst of sex" they will "perfect great bliss" (S91). If, however, one is able to utilize sexual activity properly, that is, as a controlled form of yogic sublimation, one may harness one's mental and physical energies toward the attainment of Buddhahood, a state that, in its Yoginī tantra context, involves both absolute gnosis and an experience of rapture, bliss, and ecstasy that is analogous (and even related) to the pleasure of "ordinary" sex yet infintely beyond it in its intensity, duration, and soteriological import.[31]

Is There a System Here?

The Yoginī and other advanced tantras and their commentaries often refer to the procedures involved in seeing oneself as a Buddha-deity at the center of a divine mansion, or maṇḍala, as the "generation stage" (*utpattikrama*) and the procedures for manipulating forces within the subtle body so as to completely transform oneself into a Buddha as the "completion stage" (*utpannakrama* or *saṃpannakrama*). It was understood that in both stages, stilling the mind and seeing the nature of mind as emptiness, that is, developing concentration and insight, were necessary for progress in uprooting defilements and that the final, perfected, Buddha state attained at the conclusion of the completion stage was one in which the innate gnosis of empty, blissful awareness was revealed. The completion stage, in turn, sometimes was subdivided into practices with and without signs, or into a "path of means" and a "path of liberation"; in each case, the former involved manipulation of energies within the subtle body and the latter the realization of emptiness. Because realization of emptiness—by an innate, blissful gnosis—was central to tantric definitions of enlightenment, some theoreticians made it virtually definitive of the completion stage, to the point where any formal practice (whether involving maṇḍalas or the subtle body) might be regarded as the stage of generation, and all "emptying" of those forms as the stage of completion.[32] None of the three siddhas under consideration ever refers to either stage in his dohās, yet it is quite evident that the procedures involved were part of these siddhas' ritual and contemplative world, and it is not surprising that later, systematically inclined commentators would read their verses as an instruction in the various, sequenced stages of tantric practice.

Is there, then, a "system" of yoga that is promoted by Saraha, Kāṇha, and Tilopa? On the basis of the foregoing, we might be tempted to say that if there is, it requires a focus on inward practice rather than outward ritual, and a classically Mahāyāna balance between extremes of worldliness and transcendence and of compassion and emptiness. It requires that one receive tantric initiation from a guru and develop skill in reenvisioning oneself in the bodily form of a Buddha-deity at the center of one's maṇḍala, while uttering one's speech as mantra, and keeping in mind the nondual wisdom consciousness of a Buddha. One must not, however, be content with these generation-stage meditations and must progress to completion-stage practices within the subtle body. First, one controls and pacifies conceptual thought and the breath. Then (perhaps with the help of a sexual partner) one introduces one's mental and physical energies into the central channel. Within that channel and its cakras (and again, perhaps with the assistance of a sexual partner) one manipulates mental and physical energies, and certain inherited drops, so as to induce a series of four ecstasies, the last of which, innate ecstasy, is a blissful realization of reality that is tantamount to full enlightenment. Finally, when the innate has been fully realized, then one no longer needs to control or suppress thought, but simply sees mind and the world exactly as they are and always have been: empty, blissful, pure, awake—and one goes about living in the world, compassionately and wisely.

Lest we complacently assume, though, that we now have settled what Saraha, Kāṇha, and Tilopa "really were up to" in their yogic practice, let us remember how scattered and unsystematic their references generally are, and how much guesswork is involved in trying to reestablish either the context in which their dohās were uttered or the meanings they were intended to convey. Let us also recall the often confusing mix of negative and positive discourse, the assertions counterposed with denials, that inform their discussion of nearly every topic—and their insistence that the ultimate, in any case, cannot be captured in words, and cannot be confined to any single technique or terminology. Thus, while it certainly is possible to understand their various references to mind, body, sex, and enlightenment in the way I have just suggested, we must admit that this is only one possible explanation. It is, in fact, quite possible that, in the face of achieving the ultimate, the entire raft of tantric practices I have just systematized may be a hindrance rather than an aid, and that when the siddhas sing of going beyond such things, they mean it. Similarly, it is possible that when they sing of releasing the mind to go where it will, or simply seeing it as it is, wherever one is, they mean this to be a part of the path and not just an expression of what it is like for one who has attained the goal.

At the very least, we must understand that, by their rhetoric and their indirection, Saraha, Kāṇha, and Tilopa may be warning their listeners (and us) that the crucial thing for anyone intent on freedom is simply to see and reveal the innate mind as it is. This is the value that trumps all others, and the process of attaining it has no *necessary* connection to thought or thoughtlessness; controlling or releasing mind; mantras and maṇḍalas or their absence; coarse body, subtle body, or no body; ecstasy or indifference; sex or celibacy. This is why both Indian and Tibetan Buddhists were able to discover in the dohās justifications for a "natural," even profane, way of life in an everyday laicized setting, *or* for the practice of sexual yoga and other complex tantric rites and meditations inside a tightly controlled esoteric community, *or* for tantric meditation within the context of a monastery full of celibate scholar-monks, *or* for an approach to spiritual life that—whatever one's social milieu—emphasized direct, unmediated realization of the innate mind, without any recourse at all to complex techniques. Which did the siddhas intend? We do not know. As in the writings of so many mystics, it is precisely this ambiguity in the verses of the siddhas that has made them so fruitful over the years, allowing each generation to find in them meanings appropriate to its own situation—and it is this ambiguity that we would do well to keep in mind, if we would not reduce them to the "conventional nonsense" they so vociferously rejected.

Celebration of the Guru

There is, however, one topic on which the siddhas seem to entertain no ambivalence and permit no equivocation, and that is the centrality of the guru to whatever the spiritual path might be. Saraha sings of how the ultimate is "witnessed solely / at the precious guru's feet" (S17) and adds that "if the guru's words / but enter your heart, / it's as if you've been handed / assurance" (S18). If you seek the innate, he says, you must know that "it's got from the guru" (S29)—indeed, "apart from the guru's teaching, / it's never seen" (S38). When you've managed to purify your mind, he adds, then "the guru's virtues / enter your heart" (S39). The guru's teaching is "ambrosial," and those who fail to drink it up "die of thirst / in the desert / of variant texts and meanings" (S56), whereas those who are "firmly devout / in the guru's word" will experience the wave of the innate (S57) and know that "through [the guru's teaching] / awareness is purified" (S69). However, Saraha notes, those who are willing and able to find the "virtue / in grace at the guru's feet / . . . are rare" (S95). Kāṇha celebrates the guru rather less openly but does note that the spiritual master "makes thought motionless / by the syllable of truth" (K23). Tilopa proclaims that "at the precious guru's feet / is the nondual declared" (T6; see 28a) and asks how for one "blessed at the guru's feet" the innate mind can seem unapproachable (T8), for in fact "with the guru's teaching / it enters the heart" (T31).

The only verses that seem in the slightest to impugn to power of the guru are two in which the guru's capacity *really* to teach is questioned: Saraha poses the dilemma as follows: "If the guru / doesn't explain the teaching, / the pupil won't understand—/ but the ambrosial taste / of the innate, / who can teach what that's like?" (S56a). Tilopa poses a similar quandary, in very similar words: "The real / can't be shown / by the guru's words, / so the disciple / cannot comprehend. / The fruit of the innate / tastes ambrosial; / who teaches the real to whom?" (T9a). Clearly, the "limitation" on the guru's power expressed here is only that of language itself, which never can fully encompass the ultimate. Yet to the degree that conventional speech can at least point us in the direction of the ineffable experience of the innate, it is most certainly the guru—and only the guru—who will be able to orient us properly.

The term *guru* literally means "heavy," "weighty," "serious," and in Indian tradition it has been the guru's task to inform us of the weightier truths of life, though a guru may be a teacher of any skill or subject, including mundane arts and sciences. I deliberately leave the word untranslated here because none of the possible English equivalents carries sufficient nuance, especially for the tantric context in which the siddhas use the term. A "teacher" in the West is someone who *in*forms us, without necessarily *forming* us, as a guru does. A "mentor" gives sage advice and serves as an example but does not usually bear as much authority as a guru. A "master" clearly exercises control in some way but is not necessarily either a role model or teacher. The guru, especially the tantric guru, is exceptional in the senses conveyed by all three English alternatives: as a teacher, as a role model, and as an authoritative guide. This is so primarily because the tantras—and especially advanced systems like the Yoginī tantras—provide an extraordinarily difficult and dangerous path to follow. In the tantras, as I have shown, one deals with complex meaning systems and attempts to confront and control the most basic energies and events to which we are heir: desire and anger, life, death, and rebirth. Neither the understanding of complex symbols nor, especially, the manipulation of basic human forces can be undertaken without instruction from someone who is experienced and knowledgeable about what is involved. And, in fact, because tantric systems are technically esoteric, limited to a circle of initiates, one cannot undertake their practice without initiation from a guru. If we try to do it on our own or, once initiated, ignore our guru's instructions, we almost certainly will be destroyed by the forces we seek to control—and those thus destroyed have a special circle of Buddhist hell reserved for them, the Adamantine Hell (*varjranaraka*) that is lower even than the deepest "conventional" hell, the dreaded "Unceasing Hell" (*avīci*).

Therefore, anyone who is serious about practicing tantra, especially the more advanced varieties, must find a guru who will give initiation and instruction. This is an important enough step on the spiritual path that a large body of literature exists in India and Tibet that is devoted either to analyzing the qualities necessary from both sides for a proper guru-disciple relationship or to telling stories about how gurus and disciples met and interacted. These stories, which are among the most appealing and provocative narratives in Buddhist literature, tend to emphasize above all the absolute submission that a tantric disciple owes to his or her guru. One of the best known from the Tibetan tradition is that of the reformed sorcerer Milarepa (a great-grand-disciple of Tilopa), who underwent extraordinary and dispiriting trials at the hands of his chosen guru, Marpa—including building, demolishing, and rebuilding the same tower numerous times—before the latter would grant him teachings; Marpa's "cruelty," of course, is revealed as an exercise in compassionate, skillful methods, which serve both to test and to ripen Milarepa.

This story, in turn, echoes many that are told in Indian tradition, including a number involving the authors of the three Treasuries presented here. Thus, Saraha is reported in a number of Tibetan sources to have apprenticed himself to an arrow-making yoginī, though Abhayadatta's influential collection of hagiographies tells a different, more amusing story, in which Saraha, living in the mountains with his young wife, goes into a twelve-year trance just as she is offering him some radishes. When he rises from his trance, he immediately asks for his radishes—but she points out to him that they are no longer in season, and that, besides, if he still clings to the idea of radishes, his labors have accomplished little; at this, Saraha abandons conceptual thought. Abhayadatta's account of Kāṇha similarly subjects him to gentle mockery, telling of his study under several gurus, both male and female, none of whom, because of his own jealousy and pride, he can fully obey; as a result, his spiritual progress is stunted until late in his life. Tilopa is known for having apprenticed himself to the daughter of a sesame-pounder, but is more renowned, perhaps, for his own actions as guru to Nāropa: the trials to which he subjects Nāropa before he will grant him teachings make Marpa's testing of Milarepa seem mild by comparison; they include jumping off a multistoried building, building a bridge over leech-infested waters, and abducting the queen of the realm, only to be beaten by her retainers.[33]

These legendary exemplifications of guru devotion, and cautionary tales of what befalls those with insufficient dedication, are simply ornamentation to the dohās in which, as I have shown, Saraha, Kāṇha, and Tilopa celebrate the guru as the sine qua non for practicing tantra, seeing the real, and experiencing the innate. In a modern context, the authority and devotion granted traditional gurus may seem out of place, if not downright dangerous, especially to those raised in societies supposedly guided by egalitarian assumptions. It is tempting, perhaps, to displace the outer, human guru with an incorporeal substitute, a kind of Protestantized "conscience" or "inner voice." Certainly, the siddhas would admit that the guru is more than just a flesh-and-blood human being and that in any case, the guru's instruction must be internalized and assimilated if it is to be of any value. It is dubious, however, that in the context of complex tantric practices, the human guru—and the respect one owes to him or her—ever could be eliminated, and if the unquestioning devotion displayed toward their gurus by Saraha, Kāṇha, and Tilopa leaves us uneasy, then that, perhaps, is yet another of the paradoxes that they pose for us, as surely as they posed them to their audiences in the villages of Bengal, a thousand years ago or more.

Some Differences

In the previous sections I have focused on points of style and substance on which the authors of the three Treasuries seem to be in general agreement. There are, however, some differences among them worth mentioning.

The most obvious difference is that Saraha's *Treasury* (if we include, as I do, verses attested in Tibetan but undiscovered in Apabhraṃśa) is approximately four times larger than either Kāṇha's or Tilopa's collection. Furthermore, it is by far the most ambiguous and problematic of the three texts. It contains a greater variety of verse styles, a larger range of themes, more seeming paradoxes and contradictions, and a less self-evident overall plan. There are certain "clusters" of verses, such as those critical of other religions (S1–15), those celebrating the yoginī (S84–87), or those exploring the metaphor of the "precious tree of emptiness" (S107–110) that naturally fit together, but such clusters are widely scattered, and not always clearly related to verses before or after them. These problems may be endemic to Saraha's *Treasury* because, more than the others, it is the product of a long and rather unsystematic editing process. These issues of coherence and redaction may undermine the historian's certainties about the integrity of the personage called Saraha or the text attributed to him, but for the Buddhist practitioner or for the religion scholar, it is precisely such ambiguity that gives Saraha's collection its extraordinary richness and suggestiveness. It is not surprising that both commentators and translators have been drawn to Saraha's *Treasury* above all others and that his reputation is greater, too—for within it one may find the seeds of seeing the world, and living life, in any number of different ways, from hedonistic to ascetic, from ritualistic to spontaneous, from lay to monastic, from arcane and complex to direct and natural, from tantric to transtantric.

Kāṇha's and Tilopa's Treasuries, on the other hand, are shorter, and somewhat more uniform in terms of style and content, indicating, perhaps, a less problematic process of redaction, if not absolute certainty that their current state reflects the intention of their purported authors. Kāṇha's collection contains several large and relatively systematic clusters of verses, including a series that refers to the subtle body and the various elements within it, all seen as rooted in the syllable *evaṃ* (K3–9); two series that describe the subtle body, and meditation within it, in terms of the metaphor of a mountain (K14–15, 25–27); and yet another series that criticizes conventional religious practices while exalting play with one's "inmost mistress" (K28–30). In terms of general emphasis, we might regard Kāṇha's as the most heavily "tantric" of the three collections: very little within it cannot be interpreted in terms of Yoginī tantra practices on the "completion stage," that is, within the context of the subtle body. Kāṇha details the subtle body somewhat differently from Saraha or Tilopa, concentrating on the metaphors of lotus and mountain and saying little about the four ecstasies.

Like Kāṇha's, Tilopa's collection is stylistically fairly consistent and contains a number of key verse clusters, which include treatments of the nonconceptual nature of the innate (T3–9), the inadequacies of various traditional religious practices in comparison to Buddhist approaches (T19–22), and the details of producing the four ecstasies within the subtle body (T25–28). Thematically, Tilopa ranges a bit more widely than Kāṇha, including more verses that touch on the metaphysics and ontology of the innate, and he also introduces technical terms that are infrequent or not present at all in the other two collections, most notably "unthinking," (Skt. *amanasikāra*) a meditative procedure in which one does not allow anything to stay fixed in the mind, and the "great seal" (mahāmudrā), which designates, among other things, the final achievement of the tantric path, the nature of reality that must be comprehended on that path, and a set of meditation techniques built around seeing the nature of mind just as it is and being liberated into that nature. Mediated through figures like Maitrīpa, Nāropa, and Marpa, these concepts—especially the great seal—would come to have great importance in the Tibetan traditions stemming from the siddhas.

Influences and Echoes

In General

The dohās of Saraha, Kāṇha, and Tilopa—and others whose collections have not survived in Apabhraṃśa—have, as I suggested near the outset, been profoundly influential in Indic and Asian culture. They are the direct (though not the only) ancestors of the vernacular-shaping songs of north Indian devotional poets of the fourteenth through seventeenth centuries, from Kabīr and Ravidās in the Hindi world, to Jñānadeva and Tukaram in Marathi, to Nānak and Sultan Bahu in Punjabi, to Lallā in Kashmiri, to Chandidās, Vidyāpati, and Caitanya in Bengali. To this day in north India, their images, their message—and perhaps even some of their melodies—still are conveyed by wandering yogins, including, most notably, the widely discussed and recorded Bāuls of Bengal, and their less studied cousins the Kartābhajās.[34] In Nepal, the songs of the siddhas (though diamond songs and performance songs more often than dohās) have served as a part of the liturgy of Newar Buddhist tantric priests (vajrācāryas) for a millennium and continue to shape both elite and popular conceptions of religion and of life.[35] In Tibet, the dohās inspired the development of the most personal and spiritually profound of poetic forms, the "song of experience" (*nyams mgur*), which reached an early apogee in the works attributed to Milarepa. Just like the Indian Treasuries, Mila's verse is replete with a mix of paradoxical utterances, caustic social criticism, celebrations of enlightened experience, and profound practical advice; and others followed in Mila's wake, from other "mad" yogins like Tsangpa Gyarepa (gTsang pa rgya ras pa, 1161–1211) and Drukpa Kunlek ('Brug pa kun legs, 1455–1529), to great scholastics like Longchen Rabjampa (Klong chen rab 'byams pa, 1308–1363), Tsong Khapa (Tsong kha pa, 1357–1419), and Pema Karpo (Padma dkar po, 1527–1592), to important political figures like the first Panchen Lama and the seventh Dalai Lama (1708–1757), to modern figures like Geshe Rabten and Chögyam Trungpa Rinpoche.[36]

Outside the three cultures in which the dohās have had a detectable influence, we may still discern their echoes—though they are not the sort of echoes whose causal lines may be traced but are, rather, the sort described by Rilke: "Echo answers echo: all is reverberation." There may or may not, for instance, be any but the most tenuous historical connections between the Indian siddhas and, to the east, a great and mysterious figure like the Buddhist mountain poet Han Shan or, to the west, the supreme voice of lyrical and didactic Sufism, Rumi—yet the mix of paradoxical rhetoric, social critique, and celebration of a radiant, blissful, yet ineffable ultimate are common elements in all their works. There is no direct connection at all between the siddhas and Western poet-mystics like St. John of the Cross, William Blake, or Walt Whitman, yet again, we can identify in the rhymes and in the reasoning of them all a common passion for the absolute and for attaining it in and through a human body not easily separable from the soul. More recently (and in an interesting historical development) a number of American poets in whom we also can hear echoes of the siddhas actually can be shown to have been aware of them, and in some cases specifically influenced by them: some of the earlier poetry of Jack Kerouac (e.g., in *Mexico City Blues*) was self-consciously Mahāyāna Buddhist in its orientation, with a special fondness for paradox; and some of the later work of Allen Ginsberg (by then a disciple of the Tibetan teacher and poet Chögyam Trungpa Rinpoche) looked back to Indian or Tibetan Buddhist themes of a thousand years ago and tried self-consciously to replicate their concern with expressing spiritual experience.[37] Finally, who can claim that, wherever in the world there still is troubadour trying to shake people into awareness—a young Bob Dylan or Bob Marley, perhaps—we don't still hear something of the songs of the siddhas, by an incarnation, in a new millennium, of Saraha, Kāṇha, or Tilopa?

I do not have the space here to provide examples of the various influences and echoes I have suggested (let alone those I have not). I do, though, want briefly to detail one influence and one echo. The influence is Kabīr, the echo is Blake.

An Influence: Kabīr

Kabīr lived in and around Varanasi, in north India, probably from 1398 to 1448. Born to Muslim weaver caste parents, he studied with a famous guru of the era, Ramānanda, and himself became one of the most important and beloved of the transsectarian *sants* ("saints") who were the great religious charismatics, and founding poets, of modern vernacular language religious culture in north India. Like the other sants, Kabīr often was harshly critical of the cultural status quo, and he devoted himself to interior worship of a formless God, referred to variously as Ram, the Word, the Name, Hari—or even the Innate. Like the Buddhist siddhas a half millennium earlier, he left a legacy of hundreds of songs in a variety of styles, which still are known and recited today. The form he used that most closely approximated the dohā was the aphoristic rhyming couplet called the sākhī ("witness"), of which 353 are collected in the Kabīr anthology, the *Bījak*. In those verses, we encounter many, though not of course all, of the attitudes and themes expressed by the Buddhist siddhas. Here is one in which the centrality of the guru and a critique of scholasticism and Brahmanism are combined:

> The guru's word is one,
> ideas about it endless.
> Sages and pandits exhaust themselves,
> the Vedas can't touch its limit.[38]

In the following, using a metaphor much like one of Saraha's, he expresses the importance of finding the truth within oneself:

> Why run around offering water?
> There's a sea in every house.
> If anyone is thirsty,
> by hook or crook, he'll drink.[39]

The ultimate, as "the word," is celebrated, but the inadequacies of language are mentioned as well:

> Hit by the word, one fell down,
> another dropped his kingdom.
> Whoever can discern the word,
> his work is done.
> . . . .
> Everyone says words, words.
> That word is bodiless.
> It won't come
> on the tongue.
> See it, test it, take it.[40]

As in the siddhas, mind is either criticized or exalted, depending on the context:

The mind is a nervous thief.
The mind is a pure cheat.
The ruin of sages, men and gods,
the mind has a thousand gates.
. . . .
Moving within limits: man.
Moving without limits: saint.
Dropping both limits and no-limits—
unfathomable thought.
. . . .
Make the guru your burnisher,
polish, polish your mind.
Scour, scour with the word.
Make consciousness a mirror.[41]

There even are suggestions, now and again, of a yogic or meditative technique that may distantly derive from that of the siddhas, and achieve the same ecstasy as they did:

Meditated in the sky,
opened the thunderbolt door,
saw his own reflection.
The three [worlds] filled with joy.[42]

These are only samples of verses in which the influence of the likes of Saraha, Kāṇha, and Tilopa are evident. We must, of course, keep in mind as well the differences in the setting, poets, and poems: the sants are devotees of a monotheistic God in a cultural milieu shaped mostly by Hinduism and Islam, the siddhas tantric yogins in an environment dominated by Buddhist and Hindu meditative and ritual traditions. Nevertheless, the siddhas are there in the sants, and to the degree that the sants still live in the religious movements of contemporary north India, including the Kabīr panth, the siddhas live today, too—even though they, and the Buddhism they practiced, disappeared from India almost a millennium ago.

An Echo: Blake

William Blake (1757–1827), the English engraver, painter, printer, poet, and visionary, knew of India but almost certainly had never heard of Saraha, Kāṇha, or Tilopa, whose names were barely known in the West before the twentieth century. As a seer, he wove a private mythology out of elements of Judaism and Christianity, the ideas of Emmanuel Swedenborg, and his own idiosyncratic reflections and experiences, expounding his ideas in long, visionary, prophetic poems. Blake's longer poems are difficult for the modern reader and not widely read today, but his shorter poetic works and epigrams have taken their place in the canon of English literature—and of Western mysticism. In these works, Blake decries the joy-suppressing conventions—the "mind-forg'd manacles"—of rationalism and institutional religion and exalts the imagination, the body, the senses, and sexuality. Thus, in criticism of rationalists, he writes:

> Mock on, Mock on Voltaire, Rousseau:
> Mock on, Mock on: 'tis all in vain!
> You throw the sand against the wind,
> And the wind blows it back again.
>
> And every sand becomes a Gem
> Reflected in the beams divine.[43]

Similarly, he decries three causes of error promoted by "all Bibles or sacred codes":

1. That Man has two real existing principles: Viz: a Body & a Soul.
2. That Energy, called Evil, is alone from the body; and that Reason, call'd Good, is alone from the soul.
3. That God will torment Man in Eternity for following his Energies.

Against these, Blake counterposes three true "contraries":

1. Man has no Body distinct from his Soul; for that call'd Body is a portion of Soul discerned by the five Senses, the chief inlets of Soul in this age.
2. Energy is the only life, and is from the Body; and Reason is the bound or outward circumference of energy.
3. Energy is eternal delight.[44]

He asserts, further, that both "Attraction and Repulsion, Reason and Energy, Love and Hate, are necessary to Human existence."[45] As a result, it sometimes is the case that "the tygers of wrath are wiser than the horses of instruction,"[46] and that

> Love to faults is always blind,
> Always is to joy inclined,
> Lawless, wing'd, and unconfin'd,
> And breaks all chains from every mind.[47]

Blake also is famed for his frank celebrations of sexuality, as in the following:

What is it men in women do require?
The lineaments of Gratified Desire.
What is it women do in men require?
The lineaments of Gratified Desire.[48]

Further, it is clear that, to Blake, human capacity is infinite, for he comments:

> I. Man's perceptions are not bounded by organs of perception; he perceives more than sense (tho' ever so acute) can discover . . .
>
> VII. The Desire of Man being Infinite, the possession is Infinite & Himself Infinite.[49]

And, in one of his most oft-quoted observations, he insists:

> If the doors of perception were cleansed every thing would appear to man as it is, infinite.[50]

There are, of course, many more differences between Blake and the siddhas than similarities, but the echoes of certain themes from one to the other is undeniable, and undeniable, too, is a striking formal similarity: just like Saraha, Kāṇha, and Tilopa, Blake expresses himself much of the time in aphoristic rhyming couplets. Indeed, I would argue that, if there is an English language Dohākoṣa, it is Blake's "Auguries of Innocence," which begins with the instruction "to see a World in a Grain of Sand / And a Heaven in a Wild Flower, / Hold Infinity in the palm of your hand. / And eternity in an hour"[51] and then goes on to present a series of didactic couplets, some in evident sequence, some appearing rather random. It includes many observations about the interrelations among things, along the lines of: "The Game Cock clipp'd & arm'd for fight / Does the rising sun affright" or "The Catterpiller on the Leaf / Repeats to thee thy mother's grief."[52] There also are implicit or explicit reflections on human attitudes and behavior, such as: "If the Sun & Moon should doubt, / They'd immediately Go out," and "To be in a Passion you Good may do, / But no Good if a Passion is in you."[53] There are theological observations, too, such as the verses with which the poem ends: "God Appears & God is Light / To those poor Souls who dwell in Night, / But does a Human Form Display / To those who Dwell in Realms of day."[54] I will leave the matter with a set of Blakean "dohās" that recapitulate a number of his favorite themes, and at least some of those of the siddhas, too:

Man was made for Joy and Woe;
And when this we rightly know
Thro' the World we safely go,
Joy & Woe are woven fine,

A Clothing for the Soul divine;
Under every grief & pine
Runs a joy with silken twine.[55]

About the Translation

The edition of the Dohākoṣas of Saraha, Kāṇha, and Tilopa on which I base my translation is that of the Apabhraṃśa version published by Prabodh Chandra Bagchi in Calcutta, in 1938. I have drawn supplementary material from the recent editions of the Tibetan of Saraha prepared by Kurtis Schaeffer, and of Tilopa by Fabio Torricelli. As noted earlier, it is quite obvious from reading the various available Apabhraṃśa and Tibetan versions of the Treasuries that there were a number of different recensions in circulation in South Asia early in the second millennium C.E., which (especially in the case of Saraha) only partly overlapped.[56] No editor yet has resolved all the difficulties and discrepancies among these various versions, nor is anyone likely to do so soon. Like all versions, Bagchi's edition (again, especially in the case of Saraha) is simply one arrangement of material found in a number of different forms. Like other recensions of the Treasuries, it reflects to a considerable degree editorial decisions not of the redactors of the "original" collections (let alone their purported authors) but of later Indian commentators (e.g., Advayavajra) from whose works the Treasuries have to a large extent been extracted.[57] Furthermore, though it is not unique in this, either, it contains its share of misprints. Nevertheless, Bagchi's edition does represent the one available source in which versions of all three Treasuries surviving in Apabhraṃśa have been brought together, and it contains much supplementary material that is useful, including Bagchi's running Sanskrit translation of the Apabhraṃśa texts, and Sanskrit commentaries on each from medieval writers. Schaeffer's and Torricelli's editions of the Tibetan of Saraha's and Tilopa's Treasuries are the result of a careful comparison among the various Tibetan translations, and are likely to be definitive for some time to come. I have employed them not in order to produce a "complete" or "definitive" version of any of the three Treasuries but to provide a text that reflects the dohās most commonly encountered in the "standard" Apabhraṃśa and Tibetan editions.

My basic plan is to present the three Treasuries as Indic works, so I have everywhere translated the Apabhraṃśa (usually that of Bagchi's edition but in a few instances that of Shahidullah's or Saṃkṛtyāyana's) in preference to the Tibetan, except where (as sometimes in Saraha or Tilopa) only the Tibetan is available.

Each dohā presented includes, from top to bottom: (1) the number of the verse according to Bagchi's edition, except for verses he omits; (2) a transliterated Apabhraṃśa (or Tibetan) version of the verse; (3) my own translation of the verse; (4) information (if applicable) on alternative numberings of the verse in other editions and translations; and, in a number of cases, (5) supplemental information that will assist the reader in understanding the verse.

Further explanation of each element follows.

1. To reflect the ordering of Bagchi's edition of each of the texts, I have maintained his system of numbering the verses, with supplementary Apabhraṃśa or Tibetan verses or portions of verses placed after the verse they most closely succeed in Schaeffer's or Torricelli's Tibetan version, for example, as 42a. In instances where I am not translating from Bagchi, I have italicized the edition from which I am drawing. It must be noted that in any number of cases (especially in Saraha) what is numbered as a single dohā actually is a combination of two dohās with different end rhymes and, sometimes, different themes. Nevertheless, because they have been combined as a single unit at some point in the process of redaction or commentary, I have chosen not to break them apart into their constituent units but to remain faithful in general to the numbering and grouping systems adopted by previous editors and translators.

2. The Apabhraṃśa is presented not as a definitive edition (though occasionally I have corrected Bagchi) but so the reader may have some idea of (1) the text on which I base my translation and (2) what the original might have sounded like. With regard to the latter, it must be admitted that, at our historical remove, we have only a faint sense of the original pronunciation and rhythm (let alone such melody as may have been attached), but there still is a certain value in giving the reader access even to an echo of an echo of what Saraha, Kāṇha, and Tilopa might have sung.[58] In the Apabhraṃśa, a roman-type bracket indicates an interpolation made by Bagchi himself; an italicized bracket indicates my own change. In two instances in Saraha (42d and 56a), I have included the Apabhraṃśa from Saṃkr̥tyāyana's edition for verses found in Tibetan but missing from Bagchi. Where no Apabhraṃśa is available, I have included the Tibetan, transliterated in the Wylie system, from the editions of Schaeffer (Saraha) or Torricelli (Tilopa); my occasional emendations also are indicated by an italicized bracket.

3. In preparing my translations, I have tried to remain faithful to the meaning of the original, and reasonably consistent in my use of translation terms, such that, for instance, *citta* always is translated by "mind," *jhāna* by "meditation," and so on. (On the other hand, *dhamma/dharma* is translated variously, according to context.) I have broken up the poetic line in the

translation, but in a manner that reflects the length of the line in the original. Thus, for instance, a longer line (whether of Apabhraṃśa or Tibetan) generally will merit three lines of translation, a shorter line, two. I have not attempted to replicate the end rhyme of the original—if Blake had known Apabhraṃśa, he might have been able to do so! Because Saraha, Kāṇha, and Tilopa—whatever the complexity of their meanings—express themselves in language that is direct and colloquial, I have tried to translate in an equally straightforward manner. One convention I have adopted to make the presentation more direct is to employ the second person more than is warranted by the original. Where the original speaks impersonally, or in the third singular, I have generally inserted a "you" to emphasize the point that these are instructions from a guru to an audience of disciples. Similarly, Indic languages often frame aphorisms by complex relative-correlative constructions, of the style: "Who cannot stand the heat, let that one get out of the kitchen"; I have almost invariably replaced these with conditionals that use the second person, for example, "If you can't stand the heat, get out of the kitchen."

4. My references to alternative enumerations of the verses are keyed to the abbreviations found at the beginning of the book. Where applicable, the alternative enumerations of Saraha's *Treasury* are drawn from the Apabhraṃśa edition and French translation of Shahidullah, the Tibetan edition and English translation of Schaeffer, the English translation (from Apabhraṃśa) of David Snellgrove, the English translation (from Tibetan) of Herbert Guenther, and the Apabhraṃśa edition of Saṃkr̥tyāyana. There is no alternative enumeration of Kāṇha's *Treasury*. In the case of Tilopa's *Treasury*, the alternative enumeration is drawn solely from Torricelli's Tibetan edition and English translation. When one of those sources is italicized, I have drawn my original from it, rather than from Bagchi.

5. In the notes to particular dohās, I have tried to only provide information that seems clearly implied by, or necessary to the understanding of, the original verse. Later commentators have read into individual dohās a great many details (e.g., of Buddhist tantric practice or meditation theory) that are not evident from the words before us on the page,[59] and, while aware of and interested in these glosses, I have usually chosen to ignore them, so as not to constrict the siddhas within a particular interpretive grid. I could not, however, resist noting a number of cases where there were striking parallels between a topic treated in the dohā and material found in the two Yoginī tantras that have been substantially translated into English, the *Saṃvarodaya* (in Tsuda 1974) and the *Hevajra* (Snellgrove 1959, Farrow and Menon 1992)—since, as noted near the outset, I do believe that the Yoginī tantras are the most promising single interpretive key to understanding the Treasuries.

Saraha, Kāṇha, and Tilopa never will be entirely transparent to us, as they probably were not to their original audiences. If the reader can catch in these versions, though, something of their freshness and some of their wisdom, and sense a bit better the context in which they may have lived and sung, then I will have succeeded in minimizing my "traduttorial" sense of being yet another *tradittore* to poets and sages who probably were misunderstood the *first* time around, but kept coming out of the jungle anyway, into the village clearing, to sing for the few with ears to hear, a curious heart, and a pure passion to taste the innate.

Saraha's *Treasury of Couplets*

1

vamhaṇo hi ma jānanta hi bheu
evai paḍhiau e ccauveu

Bah! Brahmins—
they don't know what's what:

in vain they incant
their four Vedas.

[G 1a, Sch 5–6]

Brahmins: Members of the highest and "purest" of the four castes (Skt. *varṇa*) of Hindu society; their traditional function was as ritual specialists, versed in the Vedas. According to later hagiographies, Saraha, Kāṇha, and Tilopa all began life as brahmins. ***what's what:*** More literally, the distinctions (Apa. *bheu*, Skt. *bheda*) a practitioner must make. ***four Vedas:*** The R̥g, Yajur, Sāma, and Atharva Vedas; together they comprise the oldest, and arguably the most sacred, literature of Hinduism. They consist primarily of songs, prayers, and spells related to various deities, and served as the major liturgical texts for much of Hindu society.

2

maṭṭī [pāṇī kusa lai paḍantaṃ
dharahiṃ vaisī] aggi huṇantaṃ
kajje virahia huavaha homeṃ
akkhi uhāvia kuḍueṃ dhumeṃ

They incant, holding earth
and water and kuśa grass,

and sit at home
making offerings to fire.

Their oblations
are pointless—

the acrid smoke
just stings their eyes.

[G 1b, Sch 7–10]

kuśa grass: A type of sacred grass, utilized in various ritual contexts by Hindus and by Buddhists in certain tantric initiations and meditative practices.

3

ekadaṇḍī tridaṇḍī bhaavaṃvesеṃ
vinuā hoiai haṃsauesеṃ
micchehiṃ jaga vāhia mulle
dhammādhamma ṇa jāṇia tulle

With staff or trident,
dressed like lords,

they pose as sages,
imparting ascetic advice.

They're fakes—
their error deceives the world;

they don't know right
any more than wrong.

[G 2, Sch 11–14]

staff or trident: Traditional accessories of Śaivite ascetics. ***ascetic advice:*** Literally, "swan-instruction" (Skt. *haṃsopadeśa*), in reference to the Hindu symbolism of the swan, whose flight mimics the movements of the soul and whose name may be interpreted as a version of the famous assertion, found in the Upaniṣads, of the individual soul's (Skt. *ātman*) relation to the cosmic spirit (brahman): "I am that" (*so 'ham*, or *ahaṃ saḥ*). ***don't know . . . wrong:*** Alternatively, and just as plausibly, this may be read as: "They don't know right and wrong are just the same." *Dhamma* (Skt. *dharma*) is a basic and virtually untranslatable term that connotes, among other things, the Buddha's teaching, the elements of existence (see K16), the way things are (see K21), the truth (see K23–24), one's social duty, and what is right, good, or proper (see S38)—usually its meaning when it is contrasted with *adharma*.

4

airiehiṃ uddūlia cchāreṃ
sīsasu vāhia-e jaḍabhāreṃ
dharahī vaisī dīvā jālī
koṇahiṃ vaisī ghaṇṭā cālī

These "saints"
smear their bodies with ashes,

and wear their matted locks
piled on their heads.

Seated at home,
he lights a lamp,

seated in a corner,
he dings a bell.

[G 3a, Sch 15–18]

"saints": The Apabhraṃśa term *airia* may refer either to a "noble" or "holy" being (Skt. *ārya*), who is securely en route to spiritual liberation, or to an *ācārya*, a spiritual preceptor. In either case, Saraha's intent is clearly ironic.

5

akkhi ṇivesī āsaṇa vandhī
kaṇṇehiṃ khusukhusāi jaṇa dhandhī
raṇḍī muṇḍī aṇṇa vi veseṃ
dikkhijjai dakkhina uddeseṃ

Fixing his gaze,
bound in a posture,

he whispers into the ears
of rich folk.

For widows and nuns
in their special garb,

he grants consecration—
for a fee.

[G 3b, Sch 19–22]

6

dīhaṇakkhajai malineṃ veseṃ
ṇaggala hoi upāḍia keseṃ
khavanehi jāṇa viḍaṃvia veseṃ
appaṇa vāhia mokkha uveseṃ

The long-nailed yogin
looks filthy,

goes naked,
pulls out his hair by the roots.

Jains mock the path
by the way they look;

they deceive themselves
in teaching freedom.

[G 4a, Sch 23–26]

Jains: Members of a religious community founded earlier in the same era as Buddhism, around 500 B.C.E. Jainism, which survives to this day in India, is noted for its strict adherence to nonviolence (Skt. *ahiṃsā*), and the extreme austerities to which its most ardent practitioners subject themselves. Monks of the Digambara order traditionally go naked, pluck out their hair from the roots, and sometimes will fast unto death. The term used by Saraha, *khavaṇa* (Skt. *kṣapaṇaka*), refers generally to a mendicant prone to fasting, but is most often taken to denote a Jain.

7

jai ṇaggā via hoi mutti tā suṇaha siālaha
lomupāḍaṇeṃ atthi siddhi tā juvai ṇiambaha

If going naked means release,
then the dog and the jackal
must have it;

if baldness is perfection,
then a young girl's bottom
must have it.

[G 4b, Sch 27–30]

8

picchīgahane diṭhṭha mokkha [tā moraha camaraha]
uccheṃ bhoaneṃ hoi jāṇa tā kariha turaṅgaha

If flashing a tail means freedom,
then the peacock and yak
must have it;

if leftover food turns to wisdom,
then the elephant and horse
must have it.

[G 4c, Sch 31–34]

flashing a tail: Perhaps a reference to the Jains' penchant for carrying a small broom with which to gently sweep living creatures from the path before them.

9

saraha bhaṇai khavaṇaṇa mokkha mahu kimpi ṇa bhāsai
tattarahia kāā ṇa tāva para kevala sāhai

Saraha says:
It seems to me for Jains
there is no freedom:

the body
deprived of the real
only gains isolation.

[G 4d, Sch 35–38]

the body deprived of the real: *Tatta* (Skt. *tattva*), which I translate as "the real," is a term with multiple meanings, including a principle, a fact, an element, or what is true, actual, or real. It is etymologically related to the pronoun *tat*, which means "that," and has important implications for both Hindus and Buddhists, who see it as an indicator of what is most real within their respective metaphysics. For Hindus, this will be brahman or ātman, for most Mahāyāna Buddhists, it will be emptiness (Skt. *śūnyatā*; see, e.g., ST 39: 9–10). The degree to which Buddhist emptiness is a thoroughgoing negation or may have positive implications is a subject of considerable debate, with tantric writers like Saraha tending toward the latter view. In any case, Saraha here is mocking the Jain concern with transcending the body; as a tāntrika, he believes that it is only within the body that liberation is to be found; as the *Hevajra Tantra* (2:2, 35) remarks, "Without a body, wherefore bliss? One cannot then speak of bliss." ***isolation:*** *kevala* (or *kevalatā*), "isolation," "solitude," is the stated goal of Jain spiritual practice, but Saraha refers here to the achievement only in an ironic sense.

chellu bhikkhu je tthavir-uesem̩
vandehia pavvajjiu vesem̩
koi sutantavakkhāṇa vaiṭṭho
kovi ciṇte kara sosai diṭṭho

Self-proclaimed
novices, monks and elders,

these dress-up
friars and ascetics!

Some sit writing comments
on the sūtras,

others seek
to dry up intellect.

[G 5a, Sch 39–42]

novices, monks, and elders: These represent three classes of Buddhist monastics: those who are probationary, or novice, monks, usually observing ten vows; those who are fully ordained, observing 227 or more vows; and those who are senior members of the order. It is from the term for the latter (Apa. *thavira*, Skt. *sthavira*, Pāli *thera*) that the name for the one surviving "Hīnayāna" Buddhist school, Theravāda, is derived. ***sūtras:*** Discourses attributed to the Buddha, found particularly in the "Sūtra Basket" of any Buddhist canonical collection, alongside teachings on monastic training (Vinaya) and metaphysics (Abhidharma). ***intellect:*** A mental process (Skt. *cintā*, Tib. *bsam pa*.) unequivocally related to conceptualization, hence used less ambiguously (and more negatively) by Saraha than *citta* or *maṇa*. See the note to S23.

aṇṇa tahi mahajāṇahiṃ dhā[vai]
[tahiṃ sutanta takkhasattha hoi
koi maṇḍalacakka bhāvai
aṇṇa cautthatatta dosai]

Others run around
in the Great Way,

where scripture turns to sophistry
and word play.

Some contemplate
the maṇḍala circle,

others describe the Fourth
as the real.

[no Sh, G 5b–6a, Sch 43–46]

Great Way: The Mahāyāna, the Great Way or Great Vehicle, the other major division of Buddhism besides the Hīnayāna; its exemplar is the compassionate and insightful bodhisattva. ***maṇḍala circle:*** In Buddhist tantric traditions, the geoemetric, concentric, palace of a Buddha-deity, at the center of which a practitioner visualizes himself or herself in order to overcome "attachment to ordinary appearances." An alternative reading would have the phrase mean "maṇḍalas and cakras"; on cakras, see the note to S24. ***Fourth:*** From the time of the Upaniṣads on, the "fourth" (Skt. *caturtha, turīya*) has stood for the highest in a progressive series, whether of states of awareness, initiations, or ecstatic experiences. In the more complex Buddhist tantras, the fourth initiation is the highest, and in many Yoginī tantras the fourth momentary ecstasy—innate ecstasy—is the state of consciousness most akin to the mind's inmost and final nature. For discussions of the four initiations, see, for example, HT 1:10; 2:3, ST 18; for correlations among various groups of four, see, for example, HT 1:1, 22–31, 2:3, 9–10, and Snellgrove 1987: 1:247–254.

12

la la nam mkha'i khams la rtog par snang
gzhan yang stong nyid ldan par byed pa de
phal cher mi mthun phyogs la zhugs pa yin

Some think it's
in the realm of space,

others connect it
with emptiness:

mostly, they dwell
in contradiction.

[no B, no Sh, G 6b–7a, *Sch* 47–49]

space: In Indian thought, especially Buddhist, a common metaphor for the objective nature of reality as empty or unlimited, and the subjective quality of the mind that experiences that emptiness; see, for example, ST 3: 8; 33:7. Space also is one of the five elements recognized in most Indian cosmologies, along with earth, water, fire, and air. In certain contexts (e.g., S34), "sky" is a more appropriate translation for the Apabhraṃśa or Tibetan original. ***emptiness:*** According to most Mahāyāna Buddhist schools, the ultimate nature of all entities and concepts in the cosmos, realization of which is required for attaining liberation. Emptiness (Skt. *śūnyatā*) may be regarded negatively as the absence, anywhere, of anything resembling a permanent, independent substance or nature (see, e.g., the Perfection of Wisdom, or *prajñāpāramitā*, sūtras, or the *Madhyamakakārikā* of Nāgārjuna); more positively, it is regarded as the mind's natural luminosity, which is "empty" of the defilements that temporarily obscure it (see, e.g., the *Śrīmālādevīsiṃhanāda Sūtra*, or the *Uttaratantra*, attributed by Tibetans to Maitreya). The critical remarks directed here at those who think "it" (i.e., reality) is connected with emptiness presumably are meant to correct a one-sided obsession with negation, which is one of Saraha's major targets.

13

[sahaja chaḍḍi jeṃ ṇivvāṇa bhāviu]
ṇau paramattha ekka te sāhiu

You may give up the innate
and fancy nirvāṇa,

but not an ounce of the ultimate
will you gain.

[G 7b, Sch 50–53]

the innate: *Sahaja*, perhaps the most important and variously translated term in Saraha's lexicon, referring to the clear, luminous, blissful, empty, nondual gnosis with which we all are born, and the recovery or uncovering of which is the fundamental purpose of spiritual—especially tantric—practice; see, e.g., HT 1:10, 15–16; 1: 10, 39, ST 3:13. In the latter verse, sahaja is described as involving an "arising in simultaneity" (e.g., of wisdom and method, or realization of emptiness and experience of bliss); it is perhaps from this that the Tibetan translation for the term, *lhan cig skyes pa* ("simultaneously arisen," "coemergent") is derived. ***nirvāṇa:*** The highest goal of sentient striving, according to all Buddhist traditions; in Mahāyāna, however, it sometimes is regarded as a spiritual dead end, a quiescence that is unworthy of a compassionate bodhisattva or a fully enlightened Buddha, each of whom is committed to continuing activity in the world. That would seem to be the thrust of Saraha's comments here, where the quest for nirvāṇa is contrasted with experience of the innate, which involves continuing engagement with the world and its objects, though without attachment to them; however, see S40.

14

joesu jo ṇa hoi saṃttuṭhṭho
mokkha ki labbhai jhāṇa-paviṭhṭho
kintaha dīveṃ kintaha ṇevijjaṃ
kintaha kijjai mantaha sejja

If you're not satisfied
in your practice,

how will meditation
get you free?

What use are lamps?
What use is offered food?

What is mantra practice
supposed to do?

[no Sh, G 7c–8a, Sch 54–57]

meditation: The term *jhāṇa* (Skt. *dhyāna*) often refers to one of a series of "absorptions" or "trances" in Buddhist concentration meditation, but Saraha tends to use it in a rather more general sense, and, it seems, interchangeably with *bhavanā*, which I translate as "contemplation," but more literally means "cultivation." ***mantra practice:*** A part of virtually every Indian religious tradition, and rooted in the general assumption that certain sounds, syllables, or phrases have a peculiar potency, such that, properly employed, they can evoke unusual states of mind or powerful forces, and affect events in the external world. They are an important aspect of most tantric practices, to the point where one of the names for the Buddhist tantric tradition is the Mantranaya, "the way of mantras," or the Guhyamantrayāna, "the vehicle of secret mantra."

15

kintaha tittha tapovaṇa jāi
mokkha ki labbhai pāṇī hrāi

What use is pilgrimage
or forest penance?

Will you reach freedom
immersed in water?

[no Sh, G 8b, Sch 58–59]

pilgrimage . . . immersed in water: *tittha* (Skt. *tīrtha*) is a common term for any pilgrimage place but originally refers to a river ford or bathing place, where purification might be attained through immersion. See T19.

15a

karuṇā chaḍḍi jo suṇahiṃ laggu
ṇau so pāvai uttima maggu
ahavā karuṇā kevala bhāvai
jammasahassahi mokkha na pāvai

Rejecting compassion,
stuck in emptiness,

you will not gain
the utmost path.

Nurturing compassion
all by itself,

you're stuck in rebirth,
and will not win freedom.

[no B, Sh 16, Sn 112a, G 9, Sch 60–65]

no B: Bagchi does not include this or the following verse in his edition of the *Dohākoṣa*, but he does include them among the uncollected dohās elsewhere in his text (IV and V, p. 48), and it is his version that I follow. Shahidullah and the Tibetan versions both place these verses here; Snellgrove relocates them, unnumbered, at the end of his translation (239). ***compassion . . . emptiness:*** The two major practices of a Mahāyāna bodhisattva are the generation of compassion and the realization of emptiness, representing method and wisdom, respectively. Both are necessary for attaining enlightenment, and the practice of one to the exclusion of the other will result in spiritual frustration; see, for example, HT 1:10, 40, and ST 33:16–18, where awakening is described as the inseparability of emptiness and compassion. ***rebirth:*** Shahidullah's edition has the virtually synonymous term *saṃsāra*, which is, in all Buddhist traditions, the most common appellation for the uncontrolled and undesirable sequence of rebirths into which sentient beings, through deluded action, cast themselves. Freedom from saṃsāra is the aim not just of Buddhism but of most religious traditions that developed in the mid–first millennium B.C.E., including Jainism and Upaniṣadic Hinduism.

15b

suṇṇa karuṇa jai jouṇu sakkai
ṇau bhave ṇau nivvāṇeṃ thakkai

But if you're able to join
emptiness with compassion,

you won't remain in existence—
or in nirvāṇa.

[no B (but see note to S15a), Sh 17, Sn 112a, G 9, Sch 60–65]

you won't remain . . . : A bodhisattva who masters both compassionate methods and the wisdom realizing emptiness will, at Buddhahood, attain nonabiding nirvāṇa (Skt. *apratiṣṭhanirvāṇa*), a condition in which one is neither stuck in saṃsāra nor absorbed in transcendental quiescence.

16

cchaḍḍahu re ālīkā bandhā
so muñcahu jo acchahu dhandhā
tasu pariāneṃ aṇṇa ṇa koi
[avaceane] savva vi soi

Hey! Give up
the lies that bind;

be free
from what leads you astray!

In consciousness of that,
there is no other;

in realization,
everything is that.

[Sh 18, G 10–11a, Sch 66–69]

that: Used here, as it often is in Hindu contexts, as a synonym for the real or the ultimate; for Saraha, as for most tantric Buddhists, it also connotes emptiness or the innate, each of which may be understood as "pervading" everything that is, and may be seen as the object of every experience and the referent of every statement.

17

sovi paḍhijjai sovi guṇijjai
sattha-purāṇeṃ vakkhāṇijjai
nāhi so diṭṭhi jo tāu ṇa lakkhai
ekke vara-[gurupāa pekkhai]

That's what's incanted,
that's what is murmured,

and spoken
in treatise and Purāṇa.

There is no seeing
that doesn't perceive it—

but it's witnessed solely
at the precious guru's feet.

[Sh 19, G 11b–12a, Sch 70–73]

guru: The external or inner teacher-mentor, whose guidance is crucial to religious practice in most Indian traditions, and absolutely indispensable in tantric traditions, where the complexity, profundity, and danger of meditative practice necessitates an experienced master and exemplar to whom one may apprentice oneself. Without a guru, one cannot receive initiation, without initiation, one cannot practice tantra, and without practicing tantra, one cannot attain enlightenment in this life—and even after enlightenment, one still owes homage to one's guru: see, for example, HT 1:6, 22, ST 39:27. ***Purāṇas:*** The class of Hindu texts, first produced sometime around the beginning of the first millennium C.E. that provide the mythological backdrop to various sectarian movements, for example, the *Viṣṇu Purāṇa.*

18

jai guru vuttau hiai paisai
ṇiccia hatthe ṭhavia dīsai
saraha bhaṇai jaga vāhia āleṃ
ṇiasahāva ṇau lakkhiu vāleṃ

If the guru's words
but enter your heart,

it's as if you've been handed
assurance.

Saraha says:
The world is deceived by lies;

the childish can't perceive
their inmost nature.

[Sh 20, G 12b–13, Sch 74–77]

inmost nature: Synonymous with the innate, and connoting the natural purity, bliss, and nonduality of the mind. *Ṇia* (Skt. *nija*) is what is natural, inborn, or intrinsic to us; it is also what is most completely our "own." *Sahāva* (Skt. *svabhāva*) is sometimes translated as "essence" or "inherent existence," and is denied by most schools of Mahāyāna philosophy, which will insist that svabhāva is just what emptiness is empty *of.* Like the equally freighted term "self" (Skt. *ātman*), however, it may be denied on an ultimate level but used conventionally, as it is by Saraha here.

19

jhāṇahīṇa pavvajjeṃ rahiau
gharahi vasanti bhajjeṃ sahiau
jai bhiḍi visaa ramanta ṇa muccai
[saraha bhaṇai] pariā[ṇ]a ki muccai

Without meditation,
beyond all renouncing,

living at home
with your wife—

if enjoying things intently
doesn't free you,

Saraha says,
how can consciousness be free?

[Sh 21 (see d), G 14, Sch 78–81]

wife: The first of many "feminine" references in the verses of Saraha, Kāṇha, and Tilopa. In Mahāyāna Buddhism, the female is a symbol of wisdom, the male of efficacious spiritual methods; in tantric traditions, especially the Yoginī tantras, the female also may represent, depending on the context, the breath-related energies that must be controlled in meditation practice, the blissful, empty gnosis that is innate to all of us, and an actual woman with whom a yogin associates in sexual yoga practices. All of these senses may be connoted by Saraha's verse, but the most general sense simply is that freedom must be won not through renouncing the world but through wise and skillful engagement with it, whether, as here, "at home with one's wife" or as a wandering yogin, who, in the words of the *Hevajra Tantra* (HT 1:6, 23–24), is "greatly merciful because of his identification with all things, roams about, uninhibited, free from social and religious convention, transcending oblations and austerities, beyond mantras and meditation, free from vows and pledges"; see ST 21:6–9.

20

jai paccakkha ki jhāṇeṃ kīaa
jai parokkha andhāre ma dhīaa
sarahe [ṇitta] kaḍhḍhiu rāva
sahaja sahāva ṇa bhāvābhāva

If it's evident,
what's meditation do?

If it's hidden,
don't measure darkness.

Saraha constantly
cries out loud:

your innate nature
neither exists nor doesn't.

[Sh 22, G 15, Sch 82–86]

neither exists nor doesn't: A classic Mahāyāna formulation of the paradoxical way we must describe things, including one's "innate nature"; it (or any entity) is nonexistent in the sense that it lacks permanent substance, but is existent in the sense that it is meaningfully predicated of some aspect of reality—or of reality as a whole. This is the famous "middle way" (Skt. *madhyamaka*) between realism and nihilism.

21

jallai marai uvajjai vajjhai
tallai parama mahāsuha sijjhai
[saraheṃ gahaṇa guhira bhāsa kahia
pasu-loa nivvoha jima rahia]

Take up what dies,
is born and is bound—

take that and perfect
the utmost great bliss.

Saraha utters
dense and deep words;

the bestial don't comprehend:
they're bereft.

[Sh 23, G 16, Sch 87–90]

utmost great bliss: One of the most important characteristics of the enlightened mind, the innate, or one's inmost nature. In many Hindu traditions, bliss is predicated of the absolute, brahman, and Buddhists, too, see their highest attainment as somehow entailing "pleasure" to the utmost degree. Tantric Buddhism is particularly notable for its description of the ultimate as blissful (see, e.g., HT 1:8, 44, ST 33:22) and for cultivating techniques that stimulate and utilize bliss—including sexual bliss—to attain that ultimate. "Bliss" (Apa. *suha*; Skt. *sukha*) is roughly synonymous with such terms as ecstasy (Skt. *ānanda*), delight (Skt. *rāga*), and rapture (Skt. *sura*).

22

jhāṇa vāhia ki kīai jhāṇeṃ
jo avāa tahi kāhiṃ vakhāṇeṃ
bhava muddeṃ saala hi jaga vāhiu
ṇia-sahāva ṇau keṇavi sāhiu

You're deceived by meditation,
so why meditate?

Of what cannot be spoken,
why speak?

The whole world's deceived
by the seal of existence,

and no one can perfect
their inmost nature.

[Sh 24, G 17–18, Sch 91–94]

seal of existence: *Bhava* (or *bhāva*), also translated as "becoming," and used by Saraha, and most Buddhists, as synonymous with saṃsāra. Its "seal" is the pleasures and enticements of the world, which make it appear more substantial and satisfactory than it really is; as Leonard Cohen puts it, "you are locked into your suffering / and your pleasures are the seal."

23

manta ṇa tanta ṇa dhea ṇa dhāraṇa
savvavi re vaḍha vibbhamakāraṇa
asamala citta ma jhāṇe kharaḍaha
suha acchanta ma appaṇu jhagaḍaha

No tantra, no mantra,
no reflection or recollection—

Hey, fool! All this
is the cause of error.

Mind is unstained—
don't taint it with meditation;

you're living in bliss:
don't torment yourself.

[Sh 25, G 19, Sch 95–98]

tantra: Here, one of the class of texts on which tantric Buddhism is founded. These are regarded by tāntrikas as having been spoken by the Buddha, in one guise or another, to his most advanced followers, and to have the same degree of legitimacy as do sūtras for Hīnayāna and "ordinary" Mahāyāna practitioners. Even tantras, though, may negate "tantric practices," where the negative rhetoric of wisdom is being expressed; see, for example, HT 1:10, 41. ***mind:*** The term *citta* has a wide range of meanings in Buddhist texts. Sometimes it connotes a bare capacity for awareness (as when it is contrasted with "mental events," *caittas*), sometimes it refers to conceptual activity (as when it is contrasted with more direct sorts of cognition, such as prajñā or jñāna). Saraha uses it more or less interchangeably with *maṇa* (Skt. *manas*). I translate this as "thought," in recognition of its rather more "conceptual" implications in general Buddhist psychology, but I'm not convinced that Saraha clearly distinguishes between them: at various times, he either disparages or exalts each of them, depending, it seems, on whether the implication of the term is conceptual mind or thought (bad) or nonconceptual, blissful mind or thought (good).

24

khāante [pivante suha ramante
ṇitta puṇu puṇu cakka vi bharante
aisa dhamme sijjhai paraloaha
ṇāha pāeṃ dali]u bhaaloaha

Eating and drinking,
enjoying bliss,

ever filling the cakras
again and again:

By such practices you perfect
the transmundane;

the master's foot
crushes mundane existence.

[Sh 26, G 20, Sch 99–102]

filling the cakras: Most likely the tantric yogic process of drawing energies (Skt. *prāṇa*) into the cakras, or nodes, that lie at the intersections of major channels in the subtle body that is within, and fundamental to, our coarse physical body; see, for example, ST 7. Depending on the symbolic system with which they are working, Buddhists will focus on three (crown, throat, heart), four (those three, plus navel *or* sexual organ), or five (those, plus navel *and* sexual organ); for fourfold schemas, see, for example, HT 1:1, 24, ST 19–31. It is through such processes that various drops are activated and controlled, and blisses and ecstasies experienced. *Cakra* also could refer to the *gaṇacakra*, or assembly circle of tantric practitioners who partake of various forbidden substances and acts as part of their ritual. See, for example, HT 1:7, 24. The Tibetan version of this verse takes the first three lines as the expression of a sensualist or literalist attitude that is "crushed" by the master's foot, that is, refuted, in line four. However, there is no evidence from the Apabhraṃśa that Saraha is setting aside these practices for criticism, and because there is evidence from other verses of *either* celebration *or* suspicion of the senses, I have chosen to read the attitude here as celebratory, since that is what the grammar seems to dictate.

25

jahi maṇa pavaṇa ṇa sañcarai ravi sasi ṇāha pavesa
tahi vaḍha citta visāma karu sarahеṃ kahia uesa

Where thought and breath
no longer roam,
and sun and moon don't shine—

there, fool, repose
your mind!
This is the teaching Saraha declares.

[Sh 27, G 21, Sch 103–106]

Where mind . . . don't shine: The central channel of the subtle body (as opposed to the "side" channels, symbolized by sun and moon), where, through various breathing, mantra, and other yogic practices, thought and breath are brought to quiescence, so that the innate gnosis, the inmost mind, may become manifest. That inmost mind may be identified either with a blissful "drop" (bindu) normally located at the crown cakra, or with an "indestructible drop" at the center of the heart cakra, where the subtlest mentality and materiality, the true basis of saṃsāra and nirvāṇa, are to be found.

26

ekku karu [re mā veṇṇi jāṇe ṇa karaha bhiṇṇa
ehu tihuaṇasaale mahārāa ekku ekku vaṇṇa]

Hey! Unify, don't divide—
don't make distinctions
in knowing;

in this whole triple world
there's one color, one:
great delight.

[Sh 28, G 22, Sch 107–110]

triple world: In Buddhist cosmology, the realms of desire, form, and formlessness, which are the most general subdivisions of saṃsāra. The desire realm consists of the worlds of hell-beings, ghosts, animals, humans, titans, and certain gods; the form and formless realms are inhabited by various deities, and attained by those who have mastered advanced techniques of concentration meditation. ***great delight:*** Synonymous with bliss and ecstasy; *rāa* (Skt. *rāga*) is the term most often used to denote the desire, passion, or pleasure that is one of three "poisons" at the root of saṃsāra, but in a typically tantric reversal, here is regarded as essential to practice, and as, in some sense, the "substance" of the cosmos. *Rāga* also may refer to the color red, commonly associated with desire and pleasure, and also frequently the color of the female deities so important to the Yoginī tantras.

27

aāi ṇa anta ṇa majjha ṇau ṇau bhava ṇau ṇivvāṇa
ehu so paramamahāsuha ṇau para ṇau appāṇa

No beginning, no end
no middle, not existence
and not nirvāṇa;

well, that utmost great bliss
is not an other
and not a self.

[Sh 29, G 23a, Sch 111–114]

No beginning . . . self: This verse is found, in nearly identical form, in the *Hevajra Tantra* (HT 2:5, 67), where it is spoken by the Buddha in answer to a question from a goddess as to what is revealed about the real at the culmination of the higher initiations of the Yoginī tantras.

28

aggeṃ paccheṃ [dahadihahi jo jo dīsai tatta soi
ajjahi taiso bhantimukka evveṃ mā puccha koi]

Front, back, in all ten directions,
whatever you see
is the real;

to be free from error today—
ask nothing else now
but that.

[Sh 30, G 23b, Sch 115–118]

29

india jatthu vilaa gau ṇa ṭhiu appa-sahāvā
so hale sahajataṇu phuḍa pucchahi guru pāvā

Where senses subside,
and self-nature
cannot stand—

that, you hick, is the finest innate:
ask for it clearly—
it's got from the guru.

[Sh 31, G 24, Sch 119–122]

self: Saraha has appropriated a term (Apa. *appā*, Skt. *ātman*) rich in meaning for Hindus. The degree to which we may read him as using the term with "Hindu" metaphysical overtones will depend on how we interpret his ontology, whether as substantialist or more process oriented, and how we interpret the usage of "self" in particular passages, whether as philosophical or everyday. Here, the usage is negative, and very much in line with "standard" Buddhist denials of a substantial self. See, however, S60.

30

jahi maṇa marai pavaṇaho kkhaa jāi
sa steng 'di na yan lag gnas
de ni rmongs pas mtshams su yongs shes bya
gti mug rgya mtsho 'chad pa gang shes pa

Where thought is dead
and breath destroyed,

on that ground
repose your limbs.

Fool! Know the in-between
completely—

know it, and you cancel
the sea of confusion.

[B (first line only), Sn 30a, Sh 32, G 25a, *Sch 123–126* (last three lines)]

the in-between: The central channel of the subtle body, which lies between the side channels; the phrase also connotes the innate, which is "in between" any and all dualistic predications, such as existence or nonexistence, self or other, this world or the other world.

31

ehu so paramahāsuha rahia [sarahem̥ kahiau] kahimpi ṇa jāi

It's utmost great bliss:
without it, Saraha declares,
you get nowhere.

[Sn 30b, Sh 33, G 25b, Sch 127–128]

It's . . . nowhere: If one ignores the Tibetan appended to verse 30 and interpolated there, this verse (minus the "Saraha declares") may be read as a continuation of the first line of the previous verse, which then would read: "Where thought is dead and breath destroyed, / That's utmost great bliss: without it, you get nowhere."

32

saa-samvitti ma karahu re dhandhā
bhāvābhāva sugati re [vaḍha] vandhā
ṇia maṇa muṇahure ṇiuneṃ joi
jima jala jalahi milante soi

Hey! Don't make problems
for self-awareness;

existence, nothingness, fortune:
hey, fool, they're bondage!

Think the inmost thought
completely, yogin:

it's just like water
mixing in with water.

[Sn 31–32, Sh 34, G 26a, Sch 129–134]

self-awareness: *Saa-samvitti* (Skt. *svasaṃvṛtti*) is used in Buddhist psychology (especially that of the Yogācāra school) to refer to a consciousness that "witnesses" acts of consciousness, hence provides a basis for explaining memory and continuity. Saraha, however, seems to be using it more generally, and as a synonym for the innate, inmost nature, stainless mind, and so on. ***nothingness:*** More literally, nonexistence, or annihilation (*abhāva*); it is used by Buddhists in contrast to existence (bhāva) but is regarded not as a solution to the problem of existence (or saṃsāra) but as a nihilistic dead end, as much of an undesirable extreme as existence. In this sense, it is *not* synonymous with emptiness, the realization of which *is* the solution to existence—and to nothingness, too. ***water mixing in with water:*** One of the commonest Mahāyāna similes for the experience of emptiness, in which empty awareness perceives its empty object so completely that subject and object no longer are distinguishable. It is similar to another metaphor for this experience, used more often by Saraha (e.g., S42a–c): making the mind like space.

33

jhāneṃ mokkha ki cāhure āleṃ
māājāla ki lehure koleṃ
varaguru-vaaneṃ paḍijjahu sacceṃ
saraha bhaṇai mai kahiau vā[ceṃ]

Meditation:
why look for freedom in a lie?

The net of illusion:
why hold it so tight?

Trust in the truth
of the precious guru's word;

Saraha says:
I've made my declaration.

[Sh 35, G 27, Sch 135–138]

34

paḍhameṃ jai āāsavisuddho
cāhante cāhante diṭṭhi niruddho
aiseṃ jai āāsavikālo
ṇiamaṇadoseṃ ṇa vujjhai vālo

From the start
the sky is pure;

looking and looking,
you only block the view.

Stopping up the sky
like that,

flawed in his inmost thought,
the fool is uncomprehending.

[Sh 36, G 28–29a, Sch 139–142]

the sky: See the note to S12. ***flawed in his inmost thought:*** As Saraha notes any number of times, one's inmost thought cannot really be flawed, but excessive conceptualizing, or even meditation, may lead to the appearance of defects in primordially pure awareness. An alternative reading of this line (adopted by both Shahidullah, 172, and Snellgrove, 229) simply says that the fool does not comprehend that the flaw is in his "own mind" (*ṇiamaṇa*).

35

ahimaṇadoseṃ ṇa lakkhiu tatta
teṇa dūsai saala jāṇu so datta
jhāṇeṃ mohia saala vi loa
ṇiasahāva ṇau lakkhai koa

Flawed by pride,
you don't perceive the real—

you ruin every way
that you've been given.

The whole cosmos
is deluded by meditation—

no one perceives
their inmost nature.

[Sh 37, G 29b, Sch 143–146]

36

cittaha mūla ṇa lakkhiau sahajeṃ tiṇṇa vitattha
tahiṃ jīvai vilaa jāi vasiau tahi [putta] ettha

Not perceiving
the root of mind,
triply you falsify the innate;

there you live
and there you die:
make your dwelling there, child.

[Sh 38, G 30a, Sch 147–150]

triply you falsify the innate: Perhaps referring to the fool's inability to understand where things arise, abide, and perish, which is, of course, in the innate. It also has been taken to refer to body, speech, and mind (Guenther 166–167); perceiver, perception, and perceived (Snellgrove 229); and ground, path, and goal (Schaeffer 297).

37

mūlarahia jo cintai tatta
guru-uvaesem̥ etta viatta
saraha bhaṇai vaḍha jāṇahu caṃge
cittarua saṃsāraha bhaṅge

If you consider the rootlessness
of the real, well,

it's revealed
through the guru's teaching.

Saraha says: Fool!
Know this well—

saṃsāric distinctions
are forms of mind.

[Sh 39, G 30b–31a, Sch 151–154]

rootlessness of the real: A common way of describing the emptiness of all phenomena. See S64. ***saṃsāric . . . mind:*** One of a number of places where Saraha stresses how fundamental the mind is to the reality we experience. The implication here—expressed in language reminiscent of that employed by the "idealist" Cittamātra school of Mahāyāna philosophy—is that the distinctions we believe to exist in the world are merely mind forms, while reality itself is unified (all phenomena being identical in their rootlessness). Cf. S41.

38

ṇia-sahāva ṇau kahiau aṇṇeṃ
dīsai guru-uvaeseṃ ṇa aṇṇeṃ
ṇau tasu dosao ekkavi ṭṭhāi
dhammādhamma so sohia khāi

Another can't tell you
your inmost nature;

apart from the guru's teaching
it's never seen.

In it,
not a single flaw exists:

it's purified,
right and wrong both consumed.

[Sh 40, G 31b, Sch 155–158]

right . . . consumed: The ethical implications of this verse are significant; it is one of Saraha's clearest statements to the effect that in the ultimate—and in one who has attained the ultimate—traditional distinctions as to what is proper (dharma) and improper (adharma) no longer apply, for in the innate one attains a purity beyond dualistic judgment. In Yoginī tantra literature, the freedom of those who have realized their inmost nature often is said to entail spontaneous and unconventional behavior, which is, nevertheless, by definition pure. See S103a.

39

ṇiamaṇa savveṃ sohia javveṃ
guruguṇa hiae paisai tavveṃ
evaṃ maṇe muṇi saraheṃ gāhiu
tanta manta ṇau ekkavi cāhiu

When you've thoroughly cleansed
your inmost thought,

then the guru's virtues
enter your heart.

Thinking such thoughts,
Saraha sings:

Tantras, mantras—
not a single one do I see.

[Sh 41, G 32, Sch 159–162]

When . . . see. This is one of Saraha's apparently "antitantric" verses, in that he seems to say that the purification of mind required for truly heeding the guru's advice is independent of studying tantras or reciting mantras. Yet tantras and mantras are themselves tools for cleansing thought, and the guru is one's master by virtue of having granted one tantric initiation, so Saraha's meaning is not entirely transparent. Indeed, the negation of tantra and mantra may simply reflect the way in which a purified mind regards them, that is, as intrinsically empty and/or as provisional means along the path.

40

vajjhai kammeṇa uṇo kamma-vimukkeṇa hoi maṇamokkhaṃ
maṇamokkheṇa aṇūṇaṃ pāvijjai paramaṇivvāṇaṃ

You're bound by deeds,
so when you're free from deeds,
your mind is free;

when your mind is free,
you reach the undeficient—
utmost nirvāṇa.

[Sh 42, G 33, Sch 163–166]

deeds: *Karma*, or action, is regarded by most schools of Indian thought as one of the conditions that keeps us in saṃsāra. For many Jains, to be "free from deeds" means to stop acting altogether; for Buddhists, especially tāntrikas, it means to be free from attachment to action; to act, but in a manner informed by insight into the way things are. ***nirvāṇa:*** See S13, where nirvāṇa apparently is disparaged.

41

cittekka saalavīaṃ bhavaṇivvāṇo vi jasma viphuranti
taṁ cintāmaṇirūaṃ paṇamaha icchāphalaṃ denti

The single seed of everything
is mind, where
existence and nirvāṇa both arise;

bow down to it—
like a magic jewel,
it grants the things you wish.

[Sh 43, G 34, Sch 167–170]

The single . . . mind: This reflects the pan-Buddhist belief, articulated as early as the first verse of the *Dhammapada*, that we and the world are a function of what we have thought. In some cases the view is taken to entail that the world and all the beings in it *are* mind, in others simply that mind affects ourselves and our world. Tantric rhetoric tends toward the former view, though this begs the question of what mind is. In Saraha's terms, it seems to be both blissful and empty, manifest in everything, yet utterly nondual, various in form, yet utterly spacelike; see, for example, ST 33:11–12. See S37.

42

cittem̩ vajjhem̩ vajjhai mukkem̩ mukkei ṇatthi sandehā
vajjhati jeṇa vi jaḍā lahu parimuccanti teṇa vi vuhā

Mind bound, you're bound—
when it's freed, you're free,
no doubt;

what binds the stupid,
quickly and fully frees
the wise.

[Sh 44, G 35, Sch 171–174]

Mind . . . wise: This verse is very similar in phrasing to S42h. ***when it's freed:*** One interpretation is that the reference here is to the meditative process whereby, having tightly controlled the mind to bring it to single-pointed concentration, one releases it so that it may roam among objects without departing from its concentrated state. ***what binds . . . wise:*** A classic expression of the tantric view that ideas, attitudes, and actions that are spiritually destructive for ordinary people, including engagement with the passions, may, at the hands of tāntrikas, be used to further one's awakening; see, for example, HT 1:9, 20; 2:2, 50–51.

42a

sems ni nam mkha' 'dra bar gzung bya ste
nam mkha'i rang bzhin nyid du sems gzung bya
yid de yid ma yin par byed 'gyur na
des ni bla med byang chub thob par 'gyur

Grasp the mind
as being like space;

as naturally spacious
grasp the mind to be.

When thought has turned
into nonthought,

you'll gain thereby
unsurpassed awakening.

[no B, no Sn, Sh 44a, G 36, *Sch 175–178*]

Grasp . . . awakening: This verse is very similar in form and content to S77. ***unsurpassed awakening:*** In all Buddhist traditions, the most common term for the supreme, complete enlightenment of a Buddha: *anuttara-samyak-sam̩bodhi*. Here, it is clearly said to result from a nonconceptual realization of the nature of the mind.

42b

mkhas 'drar byas na rlung ni rnam par 'ching
mynam nyid yongs su shes pas rab tu thim
mda' bsnun gyis smras nam zhig nus ldan na
mi rtag g.yo ba myur du spong bar 'gyur

When it's made like space,
the winds are bound;

when sameness is thoroughly known,
they dissolve.

Saraha says:
If you're able,

you'll quickly transcend
what transits and shifts.

[no B, no Sn, Sh 44a, G 36, *Sch 175–178*]

When . . . dissolve: This is a description of the process whereby, though meditating on emptiness, one succeeds in controlling the vital energies that course through one's subtle body, then dissolving them into the central channel and/or the indestructible drop at the heart cakra. Purified there, they will become the basis of one's enlightened body and mind. "Sameness" (Skt. *samatā*) is a synonym for emptiness, which is the ultimate nature, possessed in exactly the same way by all entities and concepts; it first was popularized in the *Samādhirāja*, a Mahāyāna sūtra.

42c

rlung dang me dang dbang chen 'gags pa na
bdud rtsi rgyu'i ba'i dus su rlung ni sems la 'jug
nam zhig sbyor bzhi gnas gcig la ni zhugs pa na
bde chen mchog ni nam mkha'i khams su mi shong ngo

When wind and fire
and the mighty power have stopped,

at the time when nectar flows,
winds enter the mind.

When through four absorptions
they enter a single abode,

then utmost great bliss
can't be contained by space.

[no B, no Sn, Sh 44a, G 38, *Sch 183–186*]

mighty power: Probably the earth, which, with wind, fire, and water, forms the quartet of elements that make up the cosmos and the individuals within it. Space is sometimes a fifth, containing element, and mind sometimes listed as a sixth. ***at the time when nectar flows:*** Most likely, the time when one moves the blissful drop that resides at the crown cakra up and down through the cakras of the central channel, and experiences various degrees of ecstasy, which must be conjoined with a realization of emptiness. The absorption of various coarse physical elements and mental events is a prerequisite for the ecstasies. ***four absorptions . . . space:*** The processes whereby the great elements absorb into one another, whether at the end of an eon of cosmic history, in the individual death process, or in controlled tantric meditation. The Tibetan term *sbyor* refers to a joining, or *yoga*. When the elements all have been "absorbed," then the blissful experience of the innate mind is all that remains, and is so all-pervasive that the element of space—perhaps even emptiness itself—cannot contain it.

42d

ghare-ghareṃ kahiaa sojjhu kahāṇo
ṇau pariāṇia mahāsuha ṭṭhāṇo
saraha bhaṇai jaga citteṃ vāhiu
sovi acinta ṇa keṇavi gāhiu

In house after house,
the talk is of that:

how great bliss abides
goes unrecognized.

Saraha says: The whole world
is deceived by mind,

but nonintellect—
nobody gets it.

[no B, no Sn, *Sam 128*, Sh 44a, G 39, Sch 187–190]

In house . . . gets it: This verse is nearly identical to S78. It is one of a number of places in which Saraha indicates that the real is right before us—it's what we live, see, and speak—yet it goes unrecognized because we are so easily deluded by conceptuality.

42e

srog chags thams cad kun la yang
de nyid yod de rtogs pa med
thams cad ro mnyam rang bzhin pas
bsam pas ye shes bla med pa'o

In each and every
living being, as well
the real exists—unrealized;

everything by nature
tastes the same—gnosis
is unsurpassed by intellect.

[no, B, no Sn, Sh 44a, G 40–41, *Sch 191–194*]

tastes the same: *Samarasa*, the experience wherein any entity or concept "tastes" exactly the same as any other entity or concept, because of their common emptiness; see, for example, HT I:8, 37, and the note to S42b. In later formulations of the great seal (*mahāmudrā*) meditation tradition that trace themselves to Saraha, it is the third of four yogic procedures, preceded by single-pointedness and simplicity, and succeeded by nonmeditation.

42f

kha sang de ring de bzhin sang dang gzhan
don rnams phun sum tshogs par skye bo 'dod
kye ho bzhin bzangs snyim pa chus bkang ba
'dzags pa bzhin du nyams pa ma tshor ro

Yesterday, today,
and tomorrow, too,

people insist on
the ultimate good.

Hey! It's like a hand
cupped full of water—

open up, and you lose it
and never know.

[no B, no Sn, Sh 44a, G 42, *Sch 195–198*]

It's like . . . never know: The implication seems to be that the ultimate that people seek is right at hand; unaware of the fact, though (or, alternatively, trying to manipulate or analyze it), they let it trickle away.

42g

bya ba byed dang bya ba min byed pa
nges par rtogs na 'ching dang grol ba med
yi ge med las 'chad par yod 'dod pa
gang zhig rnal 'byor brgya la 'ga' yis mtshon

To do a deed
or not to do a deed—

when comprehension is sure,
there is no bondage or freedom.

It's beyond syllables,
but claiming to explain it,

which of a hundred yogins
will point this out?

[no B, no Sn, Sh 44a, G 43–44, *Sch 199–202*]

To do. . . . this out? A classic expression of the ineffability of the real and of its transcendence of such categories as action and inaction, bondage and freedom—though comprehension of it *is*, of course, the highest freedom, and permits one to act with the greatest possible effectiveness in all situations.

42h

'jur bus bcings pa'i sems 'di ni
glod na 'grol bar the tshom med
dngos po gang gi rmongs pas 'chings
mkhas rnams de yis rnam par grol

This mind
so tightly bound—relax it,
and you're free, no doubt;

the things that bind
the deluded
are freedom for the wise.

[no B, no Sn, Sh 44a, G 45, *Sch 203–206*]

This . . . wise: This verse is very similar in phrasing to S42.

43

vaddho dhāvai dahadihahiṃ mukko ṇiccala ṭhāi
emai karahā pekkhu sahi viharia mahuṃ paḍihāi

Bound, it runs
in all directions,
freed, it stands there motionless;

look at the camel, friend:
the paradox
is clear to me!

[Sh 45, G 46, Sch 207–210]

it: The mind. This verse picks up on the theme, expressed in verses S42 and S42h, that there comes a point on the meditative path when release, rather than control, is most productive—and that, as with a camel, the result of such release will not be agitation but stillness. Also see S45, where the mind is compared to unsteady horses.

43a

kye lags dbang po ltos shig dang
'di las ngas ni ma gtogs so
las zin pa yi skyes bu yi
drung du sems thag gcad par byos

Hey, you! Look to the senses—
there's nothing
I'd exclude from them;

someone who's done with action—
in his presence,
cut the rope of mind.

[no B, no Sn, Sh 45a, G 47–48, *Sch 211–214*]

someone who's done with action: A reference to the guru, who has transcended karma, but does not thereby become inactive; rather, a guru acts skillfully and compassionately in the world, utilizing his own and the disciple's senses (among which mind is included) as a basis for liberation.

44

pavaṇarahia appāṇa ma cintaha
kaṭṭha-joi ṇāsagga ma vaṃdaha
are vaḍha sahaje sai para rajjaha
mā bhavagathavandha paḍicajjaha

Don't hold your breath
and think on yourself;

wretched yogin, don't focus in
on the tip of your nose.

Hey, fool! Savor yourself fully
in the innate;

don't just wander around,
bound by the lines of existence.

[Sh 46, G 49a, Sch 215–218]

hold your breath . . . tip of your nose: These are classic yogic concentration techniques, which Saraha is deriding as ends in themselves; divorced from a focus on the innate, they become solipsistic practices that lead to neither freedom nor happiness. In this critique, Saraha is very much in the spirit of the Buddha himself, who, if we are to believe the early *suttas* and *āgamas*, found one-pointed meditation useful for focusing the mind and attaining sublime and powerful states of mind, but did not consider it a sufficient condition for attaining nirvāṇa.

45

ehu maṇa mellaha pavaṇa turaṅga sucañcala
sahaja-sahāve so vasai hoi ṇiccala

Releasing thought
and breath,
like unsteady horses,

dwell in your innate nature,
and be motionless.

[Sh 47, G 49b–50, Sch 219–222]

unsteady horses: See S43, where the mind is compared to a camel.

46

javveṃ maṇa atthamaṇa jāi taṇu tuṭṭai vandhaṇa
tavveṃ samarasa sahaje vajjai ṇau sudda ṇa vamhaṇa

When thought has gone to rest,
and the body's bonds
are broken,

then, where things taste the same,
in the innate, you'll find
neither śūdra nor brahmin.

[Sh 48, G 51, Sch 223–226]

body's bonds are broken: One of the few verses in which Saraha seems to denigrate the body. The reference probably is to the attachment (undeniably related to our embodiedness) that keeps us bound in saṃsāra; it need not imply that the body itself is to be transcended. ***śūdra:*** A member of the fourth, and lowest, of the traditional Hindu castes, whose function is regarded as service to members of the three higher castes: brāḥmaṇa (brāhmin, or priestly), kṣatriya (warrior), and vaiśya (merchant or farmer).

47

etthu se surasari jamuṇa etthu se gaṅgāsāaru
etthu paāga vaṇārasi etthu se canda divāaru

Right here
is sweet Yamuna,
right here the Ganges sea;

right here
are Prayag and Banaras,
right here the moon and the sun.

[Sh 49, G 52, Sch 227–230]

Yamuna . . . Ganges: The two most sacred rivers of north India; in tantric physiology, they refer to the two major side channels in the subtle body, which also may be referred to as the sun and moon. ***Prayag and Banaras:*** The two most important pilgrimage spots in the Yamuna-Ganges river system. Prayag is the place, in what is now Allahabad, where the Yamuna joins the Ganges; it is the site, every twelve years, of India's largest religious festival, a *kumbha-mela.* Further to the east along the Ganges, Varanasi (Banaras) is for Hindus the holiest of all cities, a site of constant pilgrimage, and a spot where it is considered auspicious to die. Varanasi also is sacred to Buddhists and Jains, for whom it has important historical associations.

48

kkhetu pīṭha upapīṭha etthu maiṃ bhamai pariṭhṭhao
deha-sarisaa titha maiṃ suha aṇṇa ṇa dīṭhṭhao

Holy places, shrines, and lesser shrines:
all are right here—
I've been there in my travels,

but I've seen
no place of pilgrimage
more blissful than the body.

[Sh 50, G 53, Sch 231–234]

Holy places, shrines, and lesser shrines: In Both Hindu and Buddhist traditions, there exist complex systems of pilgrimage spots, designated by various terms. In both Śaivite traditions and in the Yoginī tantras (e.g., ST 9:13–27), these are counted as twenty-four, and equated with the channels, and deities, within one's body, which is "right here."

49

saṇḍa-puaṇidala-kamala-gandha-kesara-varaṇālеṃ
chaḍḍahu veṇima ṇa karahu sosa ṇa laggahu vaḍha ālеṃ

The lotus:
clusters and leaves,
scent and tendrils and colors—

give up distinctions, fool,
don't get hooked
on lies!

[Sh 51, G 54, Sch 235–238]

The lotus: A multivalent symbol for Buddhists. In exoteric traditions, it generally connotes spiritual purity, for a lotus, like an accomplished practitioner, rises above "mud" and is unstained by it. In tantric traditions, it may refer to the cakras in the subtle body, which have various channels connected to them, or to the sexual organ of the female. Whichever the referent here, Saraha appears to be warning against overreliance on it, hence probably is criticizing wrongly directed or motivated tantric practice.

50

kāmatattha khaa jāi pucchaha kulahīṇao
vamha viṭhṭhu teloa saala jagu ṇilīṇao

Desire indeed is destroyed—
ask the low-born
about it:

Brahmā, Viṣṇu, the triple cosmos—
the whole world
disappears.

[Sh 52, G 55, Sch 239–242]

the low-born: A śūdra or outcaste, a figure often idealized in tantric literature as likelier to have insight into truth than a high-born brahmin. This reading is conjectural: the phrase *kulahīṇa* may refer to someone who is without a family, perhaps in the sense of the tantric family into which a disciple is initiated. If that is so, the last part of the line might be translated: "seek there, you without family." ***Brahmā, Viṣṇu:*** In classical Hinduism, the creator and sustainer of the world, respectively; when Śiva, the destroyer, is added, they form the *trimūrti*, or three-aspected deity. ***triple cosmos:*** Synonymous with the triple world, consisting of the desire, form, and formless realms of sentient existence. See the note to S26.

51

are putto vojjhu rasarasaṇa susaṇṭhia avejja
vakkhāṇa paḍhantehi jagahi ṇa jāṇiu sojjha

Hey, child!
Study the alchemist's way,
and you stay in ignorance;

reading their books,
you don't know
the world is pure.

[Sh 53, G 56, Sch 243–244]

alchemist's way: Tantra in India was closely associated in the popular imagination, and sometimes in practice, with alchemy, which, like tantric yoga, seeks to transmute that which is most base into that which is precious.

52

are putto tatto vicittarasa kahaṇa ṇa sakkai vatthu
kapparahia suha-ṭhāṇu varajagu uajjai tatthu

Hey, child!
The real tastes wonderful—
it's something that can't be described;

it's unconstructed,
the place of bliss—
a precious world rises there.

[Sh 54, G 57, Sch 245–248]

53

vuddhi viṇāsai maṇa marai jahi [tuṭṭai] ahimāṇa
so māāmaa parama-kalu tahi kimvajjhai jhāṇa

Where comprehension's destroyed,
thought dies,
and pride is split;

there's the utmost art,
of magic made—
why bind it by meditation?

[Sh 55, G 58, Sch 249–252]

54

bhavahi uajjai khaahi ṇivajjai
bhāva-rahia puṇu kahi uvajjai
viṇṇa vivajjia jou vajjai
acchaha siriguruṇāha kahijjai

In existence it arises,
in destruction it disappears;

beyond existence,
how can it rise again?

It transcends distinctions,
and leads on to union—

the resplendent masterful guru declares:
"It's thus."

[Sh 56, G 59, Sch 253–256]

In existence . . . again? An expression of the paradoxical nature of the real, which is so intimately bound up with the world that it arises and disappears with the world's coming and going, yet at the same time is utterly beyond all such distinctions and transitions, and so cannot ever be said to arise or cease.

55

dekkhahu suṇahu parisahu khāhu
jigghahu bhamahu vaiṭhṭha uṭhṭhāhu
ālamāla vyavahāreṃ pellaha
maṇa cchaḍḍu ekkākāra ma callaha

Look, listen,
touch, eat,

smell, move,
sit, stand.

Throw off
conventional nonsense—

give up thought, don't move
from the singular!

[Sh 57, G 60, Sch 257–260]

the singular: The one reality underlying everything; whether regarded as the innate, great bliss, emptiness, or one's inmost nature, it admits of no internal distinctions. At the same time, in typically paradoxical manner, tāntrikas are able to live in the world without stirring from the ultimate.

56

guru-uvaeseṃ amia-rasu dhāvahi ṇa pīau jehi
vahu satthattha marutthalihiṃ tisie mariau tehi

The guru's teaching
tastes ambrosial;
failing to drink it right up,

you'll die of thirst
in the desert
of variant texts and meanings.

[Sh 58, G 61, Sch 261–264]

ambrosial: Or, alternatively, "tastes of immortality"; *amia* (Skt. *amṛta*) refers both to the nectar of immortality and to the immortal state itself.

56a

ṇa ttaṃ vāeṃ guru kahai ṇau taṃ vujjhai sīsa
sahaja sahāvā haleṃ amiarasa kāsu kahijjai kīsa

If the guru
doesn't explain the teaching,
the pupil won't comprehend—

but the ambrosial taste
of the innate nature,
who can declare what that's like?

[no B, no Sn, *Sam* 77, Sh 58a, G 62, Sch 265–268]

If the guru . . . like? The similarity in language and meaning between this and T9a suggests that they may represent two different Tibetan translations of the same Apabhraṃśa original, though whether it originally belonged to "Saraha" or "Tilopa," we cannot say.

56b

tshad mar 'dzin pa'i dbang gis su
blun pos bye brag rnyed pa ste
de tshe rdol pa'i khyim du rol
'on kyang dri mas mi gos so

Grasping for certain knowledge,
a fool gets
only the details;

enjoying yourself
in an outcaste's home,
you don't get covered with dirt.

[no B, no Sn, Sh 58a, G 63, *Sch 269–272*]

certain knowledge: More literally, "authoritative knowledge" (Skt. *pramāṇa*, Tib. *tshad ma*) which, according to Buddhist epistemological theory, is gained through either perception or inference.

56c

gang tshe slong na sang kha'i kham phor gyis spyod de
bdag ni rgyal po yin na slar yang ci byar yod
dbye ba rnam par spangs nas de nyid gnas pa la
rang bzhin mi g.yo btang snyoms lhun gyis grub

When begging you use
a clay cup from the gutter;

but if you yourself are a king,
what's to be done with it then?

Give up distinctions,
remain in the real—

by nature it's motionless,
even, spontaneous.

[no B, no Sn, Sh 58a, G 64–65b, *Sch 273–276*]

When . . . done? The general sense conveyed by commentaries to this verse (see, e.g., Guenther 173, Schaeffer 313) is that if one recognizes one's inmost spiritual royalty, then one need no longer see oneself as in any way lowly.

56d

mya ngan 'das pa la gnas srid par mdzes
nad gzhan dag la sman gzhan gtang mi bya

You dwell in nirvāṇa,
but beautify existence—

don't treat one disease
with the cure for another.

[no B, no Sn, Sh 58a, G 65cd, *Sch 277–278*]

You dwell . . . another: The emphasis here is on attaining a state where one abides in neither saṃsāra nor nirvāṇa, or, alternatively, partakes of both. In maintaining the balance required for such an attainment, one must apply the appropriate methods: saṃsāra is counteracted by transcendence based in concentration and wisdom, while nirvāṇa is counteracted by compassionate engagement with the sufferings of the world. If one attempts to apply the wrong antidote, the results will be unfortunate: saṃsāra cannot effectively be countered by engagement, nor nirvāṇa by transcendence.

57

cittācitta vi pariharahu tima acchahu jima vālu
guruvaaṇeṃ diḍhabhatti karu hoi jai sahaja ulālu

Abandon mind
and nonmind, too,
and be just like a child;

be firmly devout
in the guru's word,
and the innate wave will rise.

[Sh 59, G 65e–66, Sch 279–282]

child: In most Indic languages, the words for "child" and "fool" are to some degree interchangeable, since the fool is regarded as childlike, the child rather foolish. In this case (unlike in many of Saraha's dohās), the term is being used positively, for the nonconceptual state required of yogins is natural to the child—or fool. The self-characterization of yogins as fools became common in Tibetan traditions, where a "crazy" (*smyon pa*) saint was a fixture on the religious scene, as well as in later Indian traditions, where the "mad" (Hindu, Bengali *pagal*) yogin was a figure that excited considerable fascination.

58

akkharavaṇṇo para[ma]gu[ṇa]-rahio
bhaṇai ṇa jāṇai e mai kahiao
so paramesaru kāsu kahijjai
suraa kumārī jima paḍi[va]jjai

Without syllable or color
or qualities beyond,

it can't be spoken or known—
thus I declare.

How can the utmost power
be described?

Like a virgin's first
taste of rapture.

[Sh 60, G 67, Sch 283–286]

utmost power: A term with decidedly Hindu overtones; *paramesaru* (Skt. *parameśvara*) refers to the "highest *īśvara*," and often denotes Śiva. Its use here is one of a number of hints that Saraha, like many later Indian Buddhist masters, drew not just on Buddhist sources but on Hindu, especially Śaivite, traditions, too; whether the importation of Hindu terms entailed an appropriation of Hindu metaphysics is more difficult to tell: Saraha's language veers between negative and positive in its characterization of the ultimate, but this could be said of the rhetoric in many spiritual traditions—and not just those of Asia. ***a virgin's . . . rapture:*** It often is said that trying to describe mystical experience to someone who lacks such experience is like describing sex to a virgin. That clearly is the meaning here, but there is the added reference to the sexual pleasure that is both a metaphor for, and in certain senses a component of, advanced tantric yoga.

59

bhāvābhāveṃ jo parahīṇo
tahiṃ jaga saalāsesa vilīṇo
javveṃ tahiṃ maṇa ṇiccala thakkai
tavveṃ bhavasaṃsāraha mukkai

Relinquish existence
and nothingness,

and the whole world,
every bit, disappears.

When thought
remains there motionless,

you're free
from saṃsāric existence.

[Sh 61, G 68–69a, Sch 287–290]

the whole world . . . disappears: This may refer either to the general "deconstruction" of worldly appearances that ensues for one who understands reality; or to a generation-stage tantric process whereby one reduces ordinary appearances to nothing, then regenerates them as divine appearances; or to a completion-stage process where mind has been stilled at the heart or crown cakra.

60

jāva ṇa appahiṃ para pariāṇasi
tāva ki dehāṇuttara pāvasi
e mai kahio bhanti ṇa kavvā
appahi appā vujjhasi tavvā

Until you recognize
the beyond in the self,

how will you gain
the unsurpassed body?

I declare this:
Don't fall into error,

and you'll comprehend
self in itself.

[Sh 62, G 69b–70a, Sch 291–294]

unsurpassed body: This refers to the Buddha body (or bodies) that one attains as a result of tantric practice, whether conceived in terms of the dharma, enjoyment, and emanation bodies, or the indestructible vajra body. ***self:*** See S29, where the usage of "self" seems more negative; here, as in S62 or S105, the sense seems to be more positive, if not necessarily "Hindu."

61

ṇau aṇu ṇau paramāṇu vicintaje
aṇavara[a] bhāvahi phurai surattaje
bhaṇai saraha bhanti eta vimattaje
are ṇikkolī vujjhai paramatthaje

Don't think it's atoms,
or even quarks—

it's rapture unceasing
that spreads through existence.

Says Saraha:
Such error is madness—

hey, low-born!
Comprehend the ultimate!

[Sh 63, G 70b–71a, Sch 295–298]

quarks: A deliberately anachronistic translation of *paramāṇu*, which, in various Indian cosmologies, are even subtler than *aṇu*, generally taken to be as partless particles, or "atoms." ***low-born:*** I follow here the Sanskrit "shadow" (*chāyā*) to Saraha's text, which takes the Apabhraṃśa *ṇikkolī* as the Sanskrit *niṣkula*, without family, or low born. The Tibetan *ma lus dri med*, implying stainlessness, is followed by most previous translators (though Shahidullah seems to ignore it altogether; see 148 vs. 176). I cannot, however, clearly relate *nikkolī* to any other Apabhraṃśa or Sanskrit word meaning "stainless," and would surmise that the Tibetan, at this point, was translated from a manuscript of the *Dohākoṣa* with a variant reading.

62

dhareṃ acchai vāhire pucchai
pai dekkhai paḍivesī pucchai
saraha bhaṇai vaḍha jāṇau appā
ṇau so dhea ṇa dhāraṇa jappā

He's in the house,
but she asks outside;

she sees her husband,
but asks the neighbors.

Saraha says:
Fool! Know your self—

but don't meditate on it,
don't recollect or recite it.

[Sh 64, G 71b–72, Sch 299–302]

she: In this case, the "she" may simply refer to our deluded mind, which seeks the truth, or the self, outside oneself, or in mental gymnastics, when all along, it lies within, in absolute simplicity. See S80.

63

jai guru kahai ki savva vi jāṇī
mokkha ki labbhai saala viṇu jāṇī
desa bhamai havvāseṃ laije
sahaja ṇa vujjhai pāpeṃ gāhije

What the guru declares—
can you know it all?

Is freedom won
without knowing everything?

You wander the land,
collecting experiences;

not comprehending the innate,
you're in the grip of vice.

[Sh 65, G 73, Sch 303–306]

What . . . everything?: These two rhetorical questions play off against each other to express the paradox of knowledge in tantric practice: on the one hand, what the guru has to offer one—the ultimate—cannot possibly ever be fully known, at least in a conceptual sense; on the other hand, omniscience (or knowledge of the *nature* of everything, which may or not be quite the same) is definitive of Buddhahood for virtually all Mahāyāna Buddhists. See K30.

64

visaa ramanta ṇa visaaṃ vilippai
ūara harai ṇa pāṇī chippai
emai joi mūla saranto
visahi ṇa vāhai visaa ramanto

Enjoying things,
unstained by things;

plucking a lotus,
untouched by water.

So the yogin
who flows to the root:

untroubled by things,
enjoying things.

[Sh 66, G 74–75, Sch 307–310]

the root: The image of the root may be used either negatively or positively; see S37.

65

deva p[u]jjai lakkha vi dīsai
appaṇu mārīi sa ki kariai
tovi ṇa tuṭṭai ehu saṃsāra
viṇu āāseṃ ṇāhi ṇisāra

You worship a god,
and even see signs,

but killing the self—
what does that do?

Even that
won't break up saṃsāra;

short of exertion,
there is no escape.

[Sh 67, G 76, Sch 311–314]

killing the self: Saraha does not seem to be talking about suicide; his point most likely is that mindless worship of deities, and even the visions that sometimes accompany or result from such practices, are lethal to the "self" in the sense that they harm one's spiritual progress.

66

aṇimisaloaṇa citta ṇirohe[ṃ]
pavaṇa ṇiruhai siriguruvoheṃ
pavaṇa vahai so ṇiccalu javveṃ
joi kālu karai ki re tavveṃ

Eyes unblinking,
mind stopped,

you stop the breath—
so the resplendent guru instructs.

But when the flowing breath
no longer moves,

what then, at death time,
will the yogin do?

[Sh 68, G 77, Sch 315–318]

Eyes . . . do? The reference here is to yogic practices in which mind and breath are stopped in anticipation of, and in order better to control, one's eventual death; see, for example, ST 19:26–33. Such practices clearly belong to Buddhist tantric traditions, but Saraha's tone here seems ironic. He may mean that the practices described are good and important but are not as easy to practice at death time as one might think; or, he may mean that these practices are pointless because they will be of no use at death time. I am inclined toward the former; Snellgrove (233) favors the latter.

67

[jāu ṇa indī-visaa-gāma marai
tāu sai akammo pariphurai]
aiseṃ visama sandhi ko paisai
jo jahi atthi ṇau jāva ṇa dīsai

As long as the village of senses and objects
isn't destroyed,

inaction continues
pouring forth on its own.

Who can probe
so difficult a knot,

unable to see
where they are?

[*Sh 69*, G 78–79a, Sch 319–324]

As long . . . its own: Here, for reasons of sense, rhyme, and scansion, I have replaced Bagchi's version of the first two lines with Shahidullah's (150). The term that I have translated as "inaction" (Apa. *akamma*; Skt. *akarma*), Shahidullah (176) takes as "bad action." Either is a legitimate reading, depending on the point one sees Saraha as making: if he wishes to emphasize that engagement with the senses leads to spiritual ruin, then "bad action" is appropriate, while if he wishes to stress the positive aspects of sensory existence, and its relation to the active-yet-inactive innate, then "inaction" is to be preferred. Bagchi's edition (30) has *akāma*, "desirelessness," while Snellgrove (233) implies that the original is *kāma*, since he translates it as "desire." The Tibetan supports the reading of *akamma*.

68

paṇḍia saala sattha vakkhāṇai
dehahiṃ vuddha vasanta na jāṇai
avaṇāgamana ṇa teṇa vikhaṇḍia
tovi ṇilajja bhaṇai hauṃ paṇḍia

The scholar expounds
his treatise in full,

not knowing Buddha
dwells within his body.

Coming and going
aren't destroyed that way,

but he says without shame:
"I am a scholar."

[Sh 70, G 79–80a,c, Sch 325–326, 328, 330]

Coming and going: A common image for the process of rebirth that is central to saṃsāra.

69

jīvantaha jo ṇau jarai so ajarāmara hoi
guru-uvaesem̥ vimalamai so para dhaṇṇo koi

If while living
you do not change,
you won't grow old or die;

through the guru's teaching,
awareness is purified—
what wealth is there besides that?

[Sh 71, G 81–82, Sch 331–334]

won't grow old or die: In other words, if, while living, one transforms one's ordinary body, speech, and mind into the adamantine, changeless vajra body, speech, and mind of a Buddha, then the ordinary processes of birth and death to which sentient beings are subject may be overcome. This verse highlights one of the persistent themes of tantric traditions: the claim that through yogic practice, one may achieve some form of immortality.

70

visaa-visuddhem̥ ṇau ramai kevala suṇṇa carei
uḍḍi vohia kāu jima paluṭṭia taha vi paḍei

Not enjoying
the purity of things,
practicing emptiness only,

you're like a crow
sent from a ship,
who lands back on deck again.

[Sh 72, G 83, Sch 335–338]

like a crow . . . again: Indian sailors would send a crow from the ship to find land; if the crow returned, it had found none. Similarly, the yogin who contemplates emptiness without also enjoying things in their purity or (as in S15a–b) developing compassion, will not arrive at his or her destination, for enlightenment requires practices involving both emptiness and form, wisdom and method.

70a

thag pa nag po'i dug sbrul bzhin
mthong ba tsam gyis sngang bar 'gyur
grogs dag skye bo dam pa ni
yul gnyis skyon gyis bcing bar 'gyur

When you see a black rope
as a poisonous snake,
you're terrified;

so, my friends, even the upright
may be bound by the flaws
of seeing double.

[no B, no Sn, Sh 72a, G 84, *Sch 339–342*]

rope . . . snake: An allusion to the classic example used in many Indian philosophical traditions, but most especially in Vedānta and Mahāyāna Buddhism, to illustrate the way in which deluded beings instinctively misperceive the nature of reality. In this case, the mistake is to see reality as in any way dualistic.

71

visaāsatti ma vandha karu are vaḍha sarahem̩ vutta
mīṇa paaṅgama kari bhamara pekkhaha hariṇaha jutta

Don't bind yourself
to sensuous things.
Hey, fool! Saraha says:

Look at the fish and moth,
the elephant, the bee,
and the antelope herd.

[Sh 73, G 85, Sch 343–346]

Don't. . . . herd: This is one of Saraha's most unambiguous warnings that the sensory world can be a trap for those who don't know how to see and live in it properly—just as various animals may be captured or killed through their attraction to one or another worldly pleasure: the fish to bait, the moth to flame, the male elephant to the female, the bee to honey, and the antelope herd to the hunter's call.

72

jatta vi cittahi viphphurai tatta vi ṇāha sarūa
aṇṇa taraṅga ki aṇṇa jalu bhavasama khasama sarūa

Whatever appears
in the mind
is uniform with its master;

Do wave and water differ?
They're the same thing, uniform
the same as space.

[Sh 74, G 86, Sch 347–350]

wave and water: In Mahāyāna literature, especially that of the Yogācāra school, one of the commonest metaphors for the relation between mind and the things of the world, which appear to be different but ultimately are not. "Mind" for Saraha, of course, connotes the innate, blissful, empty gnosis that is our inmost nature and is, in some sense, the source of everything. This image also is known in Hindu traditions, where it expresses the relation between brahman and the manifest entities of the world. See K10.

73

kāsu kahijjai ko suṇai etthu kajjasu kīṇa
duṭṭha suruṅgādhūli jima hia-jāa hiahi līṇa

Told to whom? Who hears?
What subsides here
amid these doings?

Like noxious dust in a tunnel,
what rises in the heart
settles in the heart.

[Sh 75, G 87, Sch 351–354]

the heart: In certain versions of tantric psychophysiology, it is in the indestructible drop at the heart cakra that the subtlest awareness, the innate gnosis, is to be found. Like dust that rises and subsides in an underground passage, all things arise from and return to this deep, interior awareness.

74

jatta vi paisai jalahi jalu tattai samarasa hoi
dosa-guṇāara citta tahā vaḍha parivakkha ṇa koi

Just like water
poured into water,
it comes to taste the same:

vices and virtues
of mind, you fool—
there is no conflict at all.

[Sh 76, G 88, Sch 355–357, 359]

74a

nags la mched pa'i me bce bzhin
gdong du bab pa'i 'di ltar snang ba kun

Like a forest
consumed by tongues of flame,

all appearance
collapses before your eyes.

[no B, no S, Sh 76a, G 89, *Sch 360–361*]

75

suṇṇahiṃ saṅgama karahi tuhu jahiṃ tahiṃ sama cintassa
tila-tusa-matta vi sallatā veaṇu karai avassa

Bring things together
in emptiness,
consider them the same;

even just a splinter
of sesame husk
is sure to cause you pain.

[Sh 77, G 90, Sch 362–363, 365–366]

sesame husk: A symbol of the particulars of the world, the tiniest of which, if not understood as empty, if regarded as having self, can serve as a cause of suffering and the perpetuation of saṃsāra.

76

aiseṃ so para hoi ṇa aisoṃ
jima cintāmaṇi kajja sarīsoṃ
akkaṭa paṇḍia bhantia ṇāsia
saasamvitti mahāsuha vāsia

That is thus;
what's other is not like that:

it works just like
a magic wishing gem.

Strange, how erring scholars
are destroyed,

when great bliss dwells
in their own awareness.

[Sh 78, G 91–92c, Sch 368–371]

magic wishing gem: A pan-Indian image for a substance that fulfills all wishes. In Buddhist literature, the mind is often seen as the wishing gem, and in this case it is "that" (*so*), that is, the real or the innate, that gives us everything we need. ***own awareness:*** *Saasamvitti* also may be translated, as in S32, as self-awareness.

77

savvarua tahiṃ khasama karijjai
khasama-sahāveṃ maṇa vi dharijjai
so vi maṇu tahi amaṇu karijjai
sahaja-sahāveṃ so paru rajjai

There, every form
is made the same as space;

as by nature the same as space
thought, as well, is grasped.

There, thought is turned
into nonthought;

in your innate nature
you relish it all the way

[Sh 79, G 92d–93, Sch 372, 374–376]

There . . . way: See. S42a, to which this is very similar.

78

ghare ghare kahiai sojjhuka kahāṇā
ṇau pari suṇai mahāsuha ṭhāṇā
saraha bhaṇai jaga citteṃ vāhia
so acitta ṇau keṇāvi gāhia

In house after house
the news of purity is declared,

but outside great bliss,
it's unheard of.

Saraha says: The world
is bound by mind,

and no one at all can grasp
the nonmind.

[Sh 80, G 94a–c, Sch 377–380]

In house. . . . nonmind. This verse is nearly identical to S42b.

78a

bde gsang yan lag yongs su spang pa na
bsgom dang mi sgom dbyer med bdag gis mthong
yul gyis mtshon pas gzhan dag bsam par byed
de nyid bsam pas ma rtogs rang bzh*[i]*n 'gags par 'gyur

Secret bliss is
utterly unramified, so

I see no difference
between contemplating and not.

Some intellectualize
through the indications of things,

but they can't see the real
through intellect:
their nature is blocked.

[no B, no Sn, Sh 80a, G 95–96, *Sch 381–384*]

unramified: Literally, without limbs or branches, each of which, in Indian philosophical contexts, tends to refer to differentiation or division into parts. The implication is that reality/bliss is single, and within it (and for one who has realized it), the distinction between contemplation and noncontemplation does not apply.

78b

gal te sems kyis sems ni mtshon du 'gro
rnam rtog dang ni mi g.yo brtan par gnas
ji ltar lan tshwa chu la thim pa ltar
de ltar sems ni rang bzhin la thim 'gyur

If mind is indicated
by mind,

concepts
are held in suspension.

Just as salt dissolves
in water,

so mind dissolves
into its nature.

[no B, no Sn, Sh 80a, G 97, *Sch 385–388*]

as salt dissolves in water: A common Buddhist image denoting unity, identity, or pervasiveness, as when the Buddha remarks that, just as the ocean has everywhere the taste of salt, so the Dharma has everywhere the taste of liberation. See K32.

78c

de tshe bdag dang gzhan ni mnyam par mthong
'bad de bsam gtan byas pas ci byar yod

When self and other
are seen as the same,

what's accomplished
by trying to meditate?

[no B, no Sn, Sh 80a, G 98, *Sch 389–390*]

79

ekku deva vahu āgama dīsai
appaṇu icchem̩ phuḍa paḍihāsai

A single god is seen
in the many scriptures;

by its own will alone
it clearly appears.

[Sh 81, G 99a–b, Sch 391–392]

a single god: The Apabhraṃśa here is quite unambiguous, but the Tibetan for *ekku deva* ("a single god"), *lha gcig*, has been altered to *lhan cig*, and taken therefore to refer to *sahaja*, the innate. It may well be that this is what Saraha has in mind when he refers to the "single god," but the term *sahaja* appears in no Apabhraṃśa edition at my disposal. The whole verse has a rather "Hindu" feel to it, and a slip of the pen somewhere in the translation process, if that is what occurred, would be understandable

80

appaṇu ṇāho aṇṇa viruddho
gharem̩ gharem̩ soa siddhanta pasiddho
ekku khāi avara aṇṇa vi poḍai
vāhirem̩ gai bhattāraha loḍai

Self is the master,
all else is refuted:

in house after house
this theorem is proved.

You eat the one,
and everything else is consumed—

outside she goes,
to look for her husband.

[Sh 82, G 99c–100b, Sch 393–396]

Self . . . husband: See S62. This difficult verse seems to be suggesting that the inner self (i.e., the innate) is all there is, and that through appreciation of it, all sense of otherness is eliminated; in spite of this, people continue to seek truth in externals, or multiplicity, or duality. The third line also may be read as claiming that where the one (i.e., self) is negated, the other is negated, too—a common Mahāyāna stance (see, e.g., S96, S105). This would set the last two lines in contrast with the first two, but this is common in Mahāyāna rhetoric in general and tantric poetry in particular.

◉ 81

āvanta ṇa dīssai janta ṇahi acchanta *[ṇ]*a muṇiai
ṇittaraṅga paramesuru ṇikkalaṅka dhāhijjai

You don't see it coming or going,
you don't know it
when it exists;

the utmost power
is waveless,
and washed quite free of dirt.

[Sh 83, G 100c–101a, Sch 397–400]

◉ 82

āvai jāi ṇa cchaḍḍai tāvahu
kahiṃ apuvva-vilāsiṇi pāvahu

If you don't give up
coming and going,

how will you win
the peerless coquette?

[Sh 84, G 101b–c, Sch 402–403]

peerless coquette: The reference here is to a playful or flirtatious woman, who almost certainly symbolizes the yoginī (or ḍākinī), the multifaceted female figure in later Indian tantric traditions, who may be a symbol of blissful, empty gnosis, a visualized goddess, or an actual woman with whom one associates in tantric ritual practices; see, for example, HT 2:4, 43–50.

◉ 83

sohai citta ṇirālaṃ diṇṇā
auṇa rua ma dekhaha bhiṇṇā
kāa-vāa-maṇu jāva ṇa bhijjai
sahaja-sahāve tāva ṇa rajjai

Mind shines,
given up to the truth—

don't see changing forms
as being distinct.

If you don't break down
body, speech, and thought,

you will not relish
your innate nature.

[Sh 85, G 102–103, Sch 404–405, 407–408]

84

gharavai khajjai ghariṇiehi jahiṃ desahi aviāra
māie para tahiṃ ki uvarai visaria joiṇicāra

The mistress eats
her husband:
in a land of such misconduct,

O mother, what comes next?
The yoginī's conduct
is past compare.

[S 86, G 104–105, Sch 409–410, 413–414]

mistress . . . husband: In this and the following two verses, Saraha plays with the imagery of husband and wife, or householder and house mistress, which often are taken to symbolize the method and wisdom aspects of the Mahāyāna path. He is exalting the blissful, empty gnosis—the innate—of which the mistress, or yoginī (see S82), is the personification.

85

gharavai khajjai sahajeṃ rajjai kijjai rāa virāa
ṇiapāsa vaiṭṭhi citte bhaṭṭhī joiṇi mahu paḍihāa

She's eaten her husband,
relished the innate
destroyed attachment and detachment;

seated by her husband,
mind destroyed,
the yoginī appears before me.

[Sh 87, G 106, Sch 415–418]

mind destroyed: As in any number of other instances, the destruction or absence of mind referred to by Saraha indicates the nonconceptual state attained by the yogin who has realized, or is en route to realizing, the innate.

86

khajjai pijjai ṇa vicintejjai citte paḍihāa
maṇuvāhi re dullakkha hale visarisa joiṇi-māa

She eats, she drinks,
she doesn't care
what appears.

Hey! Beyond thought—
yes, hard to find—
the yoginī's way is past compare.

[Sh 88, G 107–108, Sch 419–422]

86a

sa gsum du yang dri med mi gnas mi 'byung ste
me ni spra ba nyid la rkyen kyis 'bar
zla ba chu 'dzag nor bu rang dbang med
thabs kyis rgyal srid kun la dbang bsgyur ba

Even in the triple world,
the stainless
doesn't arise and doesn't remain.

Fire blazes up
because of its radiance,

the moonstone drips water
through no power of its own.

Method reigns
in every realm.

[no B, no S, Sh 88a, G 109–110a, *Sch 423–426*]

moonstone: In Indian lore, a gem whose radiance is entirely dependent on its capturing and reflecting the light of the moon, which causes it to drip water. ***method:*** The "method" described here probably refers to the various spiritual skills or techniques (Tib. *thabs*, Skt. *upāya*) at the disposal of the tantric practitioner, which are believed to be even more extensive than the many methods available to "ordinary" Mahāyānists, and which give him or her control over phenomena. Alternatively, the last line may refer back to the "stainless" mentioned in the first line, asserting its skillful or effective rulership (i.e., pervasion) of things, in contrast to fire and the moonstone, which do not derive power from themselves.

87

ia divasa ṇisahi ahimaṇai tihuaṇa jāsu ṇimāṇa
so cittasiddhi joiṇi-sahajasamvaru jāṇa

Exalted both day and night,
she creates
the triple world;

it's mind perfected—
know the innate sorcery
of the yoginī!

[Sh 89, G 110bc, Sch 427–428]

creates the triple world: This apparently cosmogonic statement may be taken either as a literal assertion that there is a goddess principle behind the manifest world or as a symbolic indication of the way in which all things arise in the innate mind (of which the yoginī clearly is a symbol); alternatively, if the yoginī is taken to symbolize emptiness (as she often is), then she "creates the triple world," in the sense that emptiness is the condition for the possibility of the arising and cessation of any and all entities.

88

akkharavāḍā saala jagu ṇāhi ṇirakkhara koi
tāva se akkhara gholiā jāva ṇirakkhara hoi

The whole world
is word bound—
nobody gets past words;

but resist words,
and you'll get
past words.

[Sh 90, G 111a–d, Sch 429–432]

words: The term I translate as "words" (Apa. *akkara,* Skt. *akṣara*) is, more literally (and usually translated by me as), "syllables."

88a

snag tsha mnyes pas klag tu med
rig byed don med 'don pas nyams
dam pa sems dang cig shos mi shes na
gang nas shar cing gang du nub

Rubbing ink, you don't learn to read;
reciting pointless Vedas,
you grow corrupt;

if you don't know exalted mind
and what's not it—well, it's there
things rise and there they set.

[No B, no S, Sh 90a, G 111e–112, *Sch 433–436*]

89

jima vāhira tima abbhantaru
caudaha bhuvaṇeṃ ṭhiau ṇirantaru
asarira [koi] sarīrahi lukko
jo tahi jāṇai so tahi mukko

As it is without,
so it is within:

set unceasingly
at the fourteenth stage.

What's bodiless
is hidden in the body:

know this,
and you're freed there.

[Sh 91, G 113–114, Sch 437–440]

fourteenth stage: The stage of Buddhahood. In conventional Mahāyāna, bodhisattvas are said to traverse ten stages en route to Buddhahood, while in certain tantric traditions, this number is increased to thirteen; the fourteenth stage, then, would be the stage beyond stages, full enlightenment. ***What's bodiless:*** In Hindu literature, a common expression for the nonphysical, entirely spiritual ātman that is nevertheless embodied because of karma and ignorance; here, it refers to the innate.

90

siddhir atthu mai paḍame paḍiau
maṇḍa pivanteṃ visaraa e maiu
akkharamekka ettha mai jāṇiu
tāhara ṇāma jāṇami e saiu

I read the opening phrase,
"Let there be success,"

but as I drank my brew,
I forgot it.

I know just
a single syllable,

but, friend,
I don't know its name.

[Sh 92, G 115, Sch 441–444]

"May there be success": The four-syllable phrase that is the traditional opening to many Hindu treatises; in Sanskrit, it is: *Siddhir astu.* ***a single syllable:*** See K23. Though Saraha discourages speculation on the identity of the "single syllable" that he knows, it might be identified as the "unstruck sound" (Skt. *anāhata*), the source of all audible sounds, which themselves are associated, symbolically or actually, with everything in the cosmos. The anāhata—represented visually as a squiggle above the circle (bindu) that surmounts letters that end in a nasal (*anuṣvara*)—is taken as a symbol of emptiness, which is the source for, or the condition for the possibility of, all forms. Alternatively, the syllable might be regarded as the letter *a*, the generative syllable of the Sanskrit language, and, by symbolic extension, of all things, which is identified with the yoginī, herself a symbol of bliss and emptiness; see, for example, HT 2:4, 44; 2:4, 52. Not coincidentally, the shortest text in the Mahāyāna canon is the *Perfection of Wisdom Sūtra in a Single Syllable (Ekākṣara Prajñāpāramitā Sūtra)*: that syllable is *a*.

90a

rkyen bral gsum ni yi ge gcig
zag med gsum gyi dbus na lha
gang zhig gsum po zag pa ni
gdol pa rig byed de bzhin no

Three unconditioned, one syllable:
amid the uncorrupted three,
the god;

if you corrupt those three,
you're like an untouchable
posing as a Vedic sage.

[no B, no S, Sh 92a, G 116–117, *Sch 445–448*]

Three unconditioned . . . god: The three unconditioned are taken by commentators (see Schaeffer 335, Guenther 116) to refer to the perfections of body, speech, and mind, or ground, path, and goal, that are achieved through tantric practice. The one syllable, as suggested here, may refer either to the "unstruck sound" that lies behind all sounds—and forms—or the syllable *a*, each of which symbolizes emptiness.

91

ruaṇeṃ saala vi johi ṇau gāhai
kunduru-khaṇahi mahāsuha sāhai
jima tisio mia-tisineṃ dhāvai
marai so sosahiṃ ṇabhajalu kahiṃ pāvai

If you don't grasp
everything as it is,

how, in the midst of sex,
will you perfect great bliss?

Like a thirsty deer
who chases a mirage

you'll die of thirst,
and never find celestial waters.

[Sh 93, G 118, Sch 449–452]

as it is: More literally, "in its own form" (*ruaṇeṃ*). ***in the midst of sex:*** A reference to tantric sexual yoga practices, in which intercourse is employed to harness various energies, manipulate various drops, and effect various states of mind (most notably the blissful, empty gnosis) within the subtle body. Saraha is warning against engaging in such practices without a sufficiently profound grasp of the nature of things.

92

kandha-bhūa-āatana̤-indīvisaa-viāru apa hua
ṇau ṇau dohācchande kahavi ṇa kimpi goppa

Reflection on aggregates,
elements, fields, senses, and objects—
just water;

in these new, new
dohā verses I declare—
nothing is secret.

[Sh 94, no G, no Sch]

aggregates, elements, fields, senses, and objects: In classical Buddhist metaphysics, the universe may be summarized under a number of basic categories: the five aggregates (matter, sensation, perception, formations, and consciousness), the four elements (earth, water, fire, air, with space sometimes added as a fifth, and consciousness as a sixth), the twelve fields (the faculties of eye, ear, nose, tongue, body, and mind, along with their objects), and senses and their objects (the same twelve; if the consciousness associated with each sense faculty is added, one has another set, the eighteen spheres, or *dhātu*). In tantric traditions, all these are regarded as being, at once, empty, and identifiable with various divinities that reside in the maṇḍala; see, for example, HT 2:3, 31–36, ST 4. ***nothing is secret:*** In this and the following verse, Saraha plays counter to the common tantric concern with secrecy, and consciously or unconsciously echoes the Buddha, who often is quoted as saying that in teaching the Dharma, he holds nothing back.

93

paṇḍialoahu khamahu mahu et*[th]*u ṇa kiai viappu
jo guruvaaṇeṃ mai suau tahi kiṃ kahami sugoppu

You scholarly types,
be patient with me:
here there are no concepts;

what I've heard the guru say—
why should I declare it
in secret?

[Sh 95, no G, no Sch]

94

kamalakulisa vevi majjhaṭhiu jo so suraa-vilāsa
ko ta ramai ṇaha tihuaṇe hi kassa ṇa pūrai āsa

Delighting in
the rapture between
lotus and vajra—

enjoying that,
who in the triple world
could not have their hopes fulfilled?

[Sh 96, G 119, Sch 453–456]

lotus and vajra: In the context of tantric sexual yoga, these are the vagina and penis, respectively. They also partake of the wider polarity symbolism of tantra, relating, for instance, to wisdom and method. ***enjoying . . . unfulfilled?*** The Tibetan here gives an entirely different sense: "What for? That has no power to give truth, / so who can fulfill [through it] the hopes of the triple world" (*ci ste de bden nus pa med pa na / sa gsum re ba gang gis rdzogs par 'gyur*). Given Saraha's complex rhetoric, either might be a sentiment he would express: he might endorse sexual practices that are performed with the proper understanding of the nature of things (see S91), or he might denounce them as irrelevant to real spiritual practice, which ultimately has nothing to do with externals.

95

khaṇa uvāasuha ahavā [tatta] veṇṇi vi sovi
gurupāa-pasāeṃ puṇṇa jai viralā jāṇai kovi

The moment is
the bliss of method or
it's separately each of these;

there's virtue in grace
at the guru's feet,
but those who know it are rare.

[Sh 97, G 120, Sch 457–460]

The moment . . . each of these: This is a difficult line. Given its other usages by Saraha, as well as the contents of the following verses, the term "moment" (Apa. *khaṇa*, Skt. *kṣaṇa*) probably refers to one of the four moments linked to the four ecstatic experiences described in many Yoginī tantras: the "diverse moment" (Skt. *vicitra*), related to ecstasy (ānanda); the ripening moment (*vipāka*), related to utmost ecstasy (paramānanda); the dissolving moment (*vimarda*), related to the ecstasy of cessation (viramānanda); and the signless moment (*vilakṣaṇa*), related to innate ecstasy (sahajānanda); see, e.g., HT 1:1, 26; 1:1, 29; 1:8, 31; 1:10: 11, 13; 2:3, 6–8. These momentary experiences—resulting, for instance, from the controlled movement of the white "male" drop from the crown cakra down through the central channel of the subtle body to the sexual cakra, and back up again—may be induced through sexual yoga practices with a partner (the "bliss of method") or through a meditation on the innate that is separate from sexual yoga practices yet still capable of inducing the experiences of bliss. For various ways of reading the line, see Shahidullah 180, Snellgrove 237, Guenther 116–117, Schaeffer 336.

96

gambhīrai uāharaṇeṃ ṇau para ṇau appāṇa
sahajāṇande cauṭṭhakkhaṇa ṇia samveaṇa jāṇa

When you apprehend the profound,
there is no self,
nor is there other;

in innate ecstasy,
the fourth moment, you know
your inmost experience.

[Sh 98, G 121, Sch 461–464]

innate ecstasy: The fourth and most "advanced" of the ecstasies induced by the most complex of tantric practices. Virtually synonymous with enlightenment, it is a condition in which the blissful, empty gnosis that is our inmost nature is manifest; see, for example, HT 2:8, 31; 2:8, 33; 1:10, 15–16.

97

ghorāndhāreṃ candamaṇi jima ujjoa karei
paramamahāsuha ekkukhaṇe duriāsesa hare*[i]*

Like a moonstone
bringing light
to terrible darkness,

utmost great bliss,
in a single moment,
cancels every evil.

[Sh 99, G 122, Sch 465–468]

in a single moment: This phrase may be read as implying either that *all* evil and negativity are destroyed in a single moment of realization (a "sudden" reading of the Buddhist path), or that *the last of them* are destroyed in the moment of innate ecstasy (a "gradualist" reading of the Buddhist path). The dispute over the sudden or gradual nature of the path animated Buddhists in India, Tibet, and China and provided an important line of demarcation between and within different traditions of study and practice.

98

dukkha-divāara atthagau ūvai tarāvai sukka
ṭhia-ṇimaṇṇeṃ ṇimmiau teṇāvi maṇḍala-cakka

Suffering's sun has set
and Venus has risen,
ruler of stars;

in constant creation,
it even creates
the maṇḍala circle.

[Sh 100, G 123, Sch 469–472]

Venus: Given the imagery of the verse, the best single translation for the multivalent term *śukra*. Besides the planet Venus, however, the term refers to semen and, in a tantric subtle body context, to the blissful male drop that abides at the crown cakra and whose movement through the central channel induces the various ecstasies with which Saraha here is concerned. In a Western mythological context, Venus connotes both sexuality and femininity; in the Indian setting, *śukra*'s sexual connotations appear to be more masculine—though we must recall that in the tantric context the "ecstasy" that is śukra's nature is associated, too, with such female figures as the yoginī and the ḍākinī.

99

cittahiṃ citta ṇihālu vaḍha saala vimucca kudiṭṭhi
paramahāsuhe sojjha paru tasu āattā siddhi

Witness mind with mind, fool,
and be free
from every base view;

purify in
utmost great bliss,
and perfection will follow.

[Sh 101, G 124, Sch 473–476]

Witness mind with mind: One of the basic procedures of the various Indian and Tibetan traditions of great seal (mahāmudrā) meditation that trace themselves back to Saraha. Witnessing mind with mind may vary in complexity from a simple one-pointed concentration on the conventional nature of mind (e.g., as clear and aware) to realization of mind's ultimate emptiness, whether regarded as a mere negation of substantial existence or an emptiness that entails at the same time an experience of great bliss or ecstasy. See S102a and the notes to K28 and T33.

100

mukkau cittagaenda karu ettha viappa ṇu puccha
gaaṇagiri ṇaijala piau tahiṃ taḍa vasau saiccha

Free the potent elephant
of mind,
and don't look there for concepts;

let that vast mountain
drink the river's water,
and dwell on the shore as it pleases.

[Sh 102, G 125–126, Sch 477–480]

elephant: A common symbol for the mind in Buddhist discussions of meditation. Here, the image is used positively, but see the next verse, where it is a symbol of uncontrolled senses, and K25, where it apparently stands for conceptual thought, which must be overcome in any serious meditation practice.

101

visaa-gaendeṃ kareṃ gahia jima mārai paḍihāi
joi kavaḍiāra jima tima taho ṇissari jāi

Seized
by the elephant trunk of senses,
he seems to die,

but the yogin,
like a skillful trainer,
escapes and goes away.

[Sh 103, G 127–128, Sch 481–484]

102

jo bhava so ṇivvāṇa khalu sa uṇa maṇṇahu aṇṇa
ekka sahāveṃ virahia ṇimmala maiṃ paḍivaṇṇa

Existence is nirvāṇa—
indeed, they can't be
considered apart;

they lack a single nature—
to me they are
completely stainless.

[Sh 104, G 129, Sch 485–488]

they lack a single nature: An alternative reading would be: "one, lacking any nature." As in so many instances, either reading is plausible in the context of Saraha's rhetoric, in which a concept like oneness may be either affirmed or denied, depending on the point that he wishes to make; see, for example, S80, where a similar ambiguity seems to be at work.

102a

yid *[kyi]* de nyid dmigs dang bcas
dmigs *[med]* stong pa nyid yin la
gnyis la skyon ni yod pa ste
rnal 'byor gang gis sgom pa min

The real nature of thought
is the referent, the nonreferent
is emptiness;

the flaw is in duality—
there is no yogin
who meditates upon it.

[no B, Sh 104a, G 130–132, *Sch 489–492*]

the referent, the nonreferent: This and the following verse employ epistemological terminology somewhat unusual in Saraha. A "referent" (Tib. *dmigs*, Skt. *ālambana*) is a "support" for meditation or, more broadly, an intentional object. The point in both verses is that true meditation (which ultimately is indistinguishable from nonmeditation), may conventionally be said to have a referent (the real nature of thought) but that the actual nature of that referent (which is emptiness and bliss) places it beyond any reference whatsoever, into an ineffable realm that only can be approached through one's guru.

102b

sgom pa dmigs bcas dmigs med de
sgom dang mi sgom tha snyad med
bde ba'i rnam pa'i rang bzhin no
rab tu bla med rang 'byung ba
bla ma'i dus thabs bsten pas shes

Meditation lacks
referent or referring;
meditation and nonmeditation

do not differ—
by nature, they're aspects of bliss.

What's utterly unsurpassed and self-arising,
is known in reliance
on a guru's timely means.

[no B, Sh 104a, G 130–132, *Sch 493–497*]

103

gharahi ma thakku ma jāhi vaṇe jahi tahi maṇa pariāṇa
saalu ṇirantara vohi-ṭhia kahiṃ bhava kahiṃ ṇivvāṇa

Don't stay at home,
don't go to the forest,
just recognize mind wherever you are;

all is unceasingly fixed
in awakening,
so where is existence, where is nirvāṇa?

[Sh 105, G 133, Sch 498–501]

awakening: The original here is *vohi* (Skt. *bodhi*), the most common Buddhist term for enlightenment; *bodhi, buddha*, and *buddhi* (intelligence) all are derivatives of the Sanskrit verbal root *budh*, meaning to awaken.

103a

yid kyi dri ma dag la lhan cig skyes pa ste
de tshe mi mthun phyogs kyis 'jug pa med
ji ltar rgya mtsho dang bar gyur pa la
chu bur chu nyid yin te de nyid thim par 'gyur

When thought is purified of stains,
that is the innate,

where what's improper
won't enter in—

just as in the ocean's midst,
bubbles are only water,

dissolving into
just that.

[no B, Sh 105a, G 134–135b, *Sch 502–505*]

what's improper: See S38, where the innate is said to transcend proper and improper, whereas here it is said to assure propriety. The two verses are not, however, contradictory, for the true propriety entailed by the innate must transcend dualities, including that of proper and improper, while the attainment that is gained through realization of the innate could not possibly admit of impropriety in any meaningful sense, since the innate, as said in S38, is by nature "purified."

104

ṇau ghare ṇau vaṇeṃ vohi ṭhiu ehu pariāṇahu bheu
nimmala-citta-sahāvatā karahu avikala seu

Awakening's not at home
and not in the forest—
you must recognize what's what;

bring forth
the stainless nature of mind,
quite beyond concepts.

[Sh 106, G 135c–136b, Sch 506–509]

105

ehu so appā ehu paru jo paribhāvai kovi
teṃ viṇu vandhe veṭṭhi kiu appa vimukkau tovi

"This is self,
and this is other"—
who is thusly circumscribed?

You're unbound!
The self that's been encompassed
is released.

[Sh 107, G 136c–137b, Sch 510–513]

106

para appāṇa ma bhanti karu saala nirantara vuddha
ehu se ṇimmala paramapau cittasahāveṃ suddha

Don't be confused
about other and self:
all are unceasingly Buddha;

that's it:
the stainless utmost place,
mind quite naturally pure.

[Sh 108, G 137c–138, Sch 514–517]

Don't . . . pure: See T13, to which this is nearly identical. ***Buddha:*** Alternatively, this term may be taken adjectivally as meaning "awake" or "enlightened," each of which is a common translation of the term.

107

addaa citta-taruaraha gau tihuvaneṃ vitthāra
karuṇā phullīphala dharai ṇāu paratta ūāra

The precious tree
of nondual mind
spreads through the triple world;

it bears compassion flower and fruit,
though there is no other
or doing good.

[Sh 109, G 139–140, Sch 518–521]

The precious . . . good: This verse is identical to T12, below. ***tree:*** A rich and ambiguous symbol in Indian culture and religion. In the Vedas, it is a symbol of life. In the Upanisads, brahman is likened to a great inverted fig tree, with its roots in the sky and its branches here below. The *Bhagavad Gītā* (15:2–3) speaks of the need to fell the tree of sense and action with the axe of non-attachment. Buddhists will, of course, recollect the tree under which the Buddha attained enlightenment. In the songs of the siddhas, the tree is often likened to the mind, sometimes, as here, in its ultimate nature or attainment, sometimes in its relative, dualistic aspect, which must be cut down. ***though there is . . . good:*** I follow Bagchi's edition here, and read *ṇāu* (Skt. *nāsti*), "is no," rather than (as Shahidullah has it, p. 164) *ṇāme* (Skt. *nāma*), "its name is." The latter reading would change the meaning of the last line to: "it bears compassion flower and fruit, and its name is doing good for others." The Tibetan supports Shahidullah's reading. As before, either version reflects a sentiment Saraha could have expressed.

108

suṇṇa taruvara phulliau karuṇā viviha vicitta
aṇṇā bhoa parattaphalu ehu sokkha paru citta

The precious tree of emptiness
blooms compassion,
various and many hued;

another's pleasure
is its final fruit: mind
intent on others' joy.

[Sh 110 (Tib. only), G 141, Sch 522–525]

109

suṇṇa taruvara ṇikkaruṇa jahi puṇu mūla ṇa sāha
tahi ālamūla jo karai tasu paḍibhajjāi vāha

The precious tree of emptiness
lacks compassion;
it has no root or branches,

so if you prattle about it,
your troubles
will only grow.

[Sh 111 (Tib. only), G 142, Sch 526–529]

110

ekkemvī ekkevi taru teṃ kāraṇe phala ekka
e abhiṇṇā jo muṇai so bhavaṇivvāṇa vimukka

It's just one,
just one tree—
that's why the fruit is one.

Knowing it can't be split,
you're free from existence—
and from nirvāṇa.

[Sh 12 (Tib. only), G 143, Sch 530–533]

111

jo atthīaṇa ṭhīaū so jai jāi ṇirāsa
khaṇḍasarāveṃ bhikkha varu cchaḍahu e gihavāsa

A supplicant
may go away
with hopes unfulfilled,

or with alms
in a broken bowl—it's better
to throw out the owner.

[Sh 113 (Tib. only), G 144, Sch 534–537]

the owner: Literally, the house dweller; the reference probably is to the sense of ownership, and the self-cherishing attitude at the root that, no matter what one's level of spiritual development, is an impediment to freedom. From the Buddhist point of view, of course, there really is no owner, for, when we search for a self, we find that "nobody's home."

112

paraūāra ṇa kiaū atthi ṇa dīau dāṇa
ehu saṃsare kavaṇa phalu varu chaḍḍahu appāṇa

Not working for others' sake,
not giving
to those in need:

well, there's the fruit
of saṃsāra—it's better
to throw out the self.

[Sh 114 (Tib. only), G 145, Sch 538–541]

Not working . . . saṃsāra: Although selfishness is described here as a fruit, or result, of saṃsāra, it equally may be regarded as its cause, since it is the self-cherishing attitude, rooted in the mistaken apprehension of a subsisting self, that is root of all the defilements and tainted actions that propel the wheel of existence onward.

Kāṇha's *Treasury of Couplets*

1

loaha gavva samuvvahai hauṃ paramatthe pavīṇa
koḍiha majjheṃ ekku jai hoi ṇirañjaṇa-līṇa

Worldlings display
their arrogance:
"I've entered the ultimate!"

But if one
in ten million
is tied to the unadorned . . .

the unadorned: Alternatively, "the naked," or "unclothed" (Skt. *nirañjana*, Tib. *ma gos pa*). In either case, it means reality as it is, uncomplicated by any conceptual elaboration or dualistic speculation. As Shahidullah notes (89), the term refers to God in many modern Indian languages.

2

āgama-vea-purāṇeṃ paṇḍiā māṇa vahanti
pakka siriphale alia jima vāheria bhamanti

Scholars put pride
in their scriptures,
Vedas, and Purāṇas;

they circle outside
like bees
round a ripened fruit.

3

vohicia raabhūsia akkohehiṃ siṭṭhao
pokkharavia sahāva suha ṇia-dehahi diṭṭhao

The awakening mind,
caked with dust, is covered
by the unmoving;

natural bliss is seen,
like a lotus,
in your inmost body.

awakening mind: The bodhicitta (Apa. *vohicia*) is, in a Mahāyāna context, the aspiration to attain enlightenment, or awakening, for the sake of all beings. This meaning is preserved in tantric traditions, where it also may refer, in the context of subtle body practices, to the blissful white drop that resides at the crown cakra or, more broadly, to the innate. The implication seems to be that the bodhicitta is not evident to us but resides within the unchanging nature of reality. Alternatively, the reference to the unmoving may imply that the bodhicitta (which in a tantric context must be stabilized) itself is unmoving. ***inmost body:*** Probably a reference to the subtle body. An equally plausible translation is: "your own body."

4

gaaṇa ṇīra amiāha pāṃka mūla-vajja bhāviai
avadhūi-kia mūlaṇāla haṃkāro vi jāai

Space is the water,
infinite light the mud—
it's without a root;

the central channel's the basic stalk,
the syllable Haṃ
the blossom.

Haṃ: The syllable generally associated in Buddhist tantra with the white drop at the crown cakra, the nature of which is great bliss. The verse as a whole is a description of the subtle body using the imagery of the lotus. In addition to the subtle body as a whole, though, the lotus also may be used to symbolize the cakras within the subtle body, or—as in K3—the supreme purity residing within those cakras, that is, one's innate blissful, empty gnosis.

5

lalaṇā rasaṇā ravi sasi tuḍia veṇṇa vi pāse
patto-cauṭṭha caumūṇāla ṭhia mahāsuha vāse

The left and right channels,
the sun and moon,
are stopped on either side;

the four leaves,
and the four roots:
great bliss resides within!

the four leaves and the four roots: The four leaves and roots may refer to the four major lotuses, that is, cakras, in the central channel of the subtle body; they may also refer to the four ecstasies that are experienced within the central channel, as well as to any number of fourfold schemes that parallel those four, from the four initiations of the Yoginī tantras, to four emptinesses, four luminosities, four moments, four Buddha bodies, etc. See note to S11.

6

evaṃkāra via laia kusumiaaravindae
mahuara-rūeṃ suraa-vīra jiṃghai maarandae

Sprung from
the Evaṃkāra seed,
the lotus is in bloom;

the rapturous hero
sips its pollen
like a bee.

Evaṃkāra: *Evaṃ* ("thus") is the first word of any Indic language Buddhist sūtra or tantra, part of the standard phrase "Thus I have heard at one time" (*evaṃ mayā śrutam ekāsmin samaye*), and in tantric circles came to be regarded as a mantra that symbolized the source or basic substance ("seed") of all things. It sometimes was divided into its component syllables, *e* and *vaṃ*, which were taken to represent, among other things, the wisdom realizing emptiness and the experience of great bliss; the conjoining of the two indicates the qualities of the innate gnosis that is the inmost nature of the mind; as the *Hevajra Tantra* says (HT 2:3, 4), "It is there that the ecstasies arise." See also ST 3:17, where *evaṃ* is said to be the locus of the experience of Buddhahood. *Evaṃkāra* means "that which effects *evaṃ*," or simply "the syllable *evaṃ*."

7

pañca mahābhūā via lai sāmaggie jaia
pūhavi ava tea gaṃdhavaha gaaṇa sañjaia

Based on that seed,
all the five
great elements rise:

solid and liquid,
brilliance and breeze—
all arise from space.

space: As I have shown (note to S12), space is a common symbol for emptiness; to the degree that emptiness is the "source," or condition for the possibility, of all forms, so, too, space is the source of all the other elements.

8

gaaṇa-samīraṇa-suhavāse pañcehiṃ paripuṇṇae
saala surāsura ehu uatti vaḍhie ehu so suṇṇae

The place of space,
and wind, and bliss,
is filled with the five;

all the gods and titans
proceed from that—
and that, fool, is empty.

the five: the five great elements: earth, water, fire, wind, and space. The image here is of the basic reality, the innate gnosis ("space, wind, and bliss," or emptiness, vital energy, and bliss) generating the five basic elements, which, in turn, become the source of all beings—but one must recall that the source itself is empty.

9

khiti jala jalaṇa pavaṇa gaaṇa vi māṇaha
maṇḍala-cakka visaavuddhi lai parimāṇaha

Earth, water,
fire, wind, space:
think on them!

The maṇḍala circle:
knowing how things are,
understand it.

maṇḍala circle: See K18. The maṇḍala circle itself is regarded as a purified transformation of the five great elements.

10

ṇittaraṅga sama sahaja-rūa saala-kalusa-virahie
pāpa-puṇṇarahie kuccha ṇāhi kāṇhu phuḍa kahie

Waveless and ever the same,
the form of the innate
is without defilement;

in it, there is
no vice or virtue at all,
Kāṇha plainly declares.

waveless: See S72, where at least a provisional distinction is suggested between water and waves. See also S81, where the "utmost power" is described as waveless, and HT 1:10, 32, where utmost rapture (*paramarati*) is described as "waveless." ***virtue:*** *Puṇṇa* (Skt. *puṇya*) often is translated as "merit," but in Buddhist discourse it is one of the most common terms for that which is ethically positive, hence a good candidate for a Buddhist equivalent of the Western philosophical concept of "virtue" or "goodness"—with the understanding that virtue is not an abstraction or Platonic idea but a term applied to particular actions that entail positive results.

11

vahiṇṇikkaliā kaliā suṇṇāsuṇṇa paiṭṭha
suṇṇāsuṇṇa veṇṇi majjheṃ re vaḍha kimpi ṇa diṭṭha

Go outside, look around,
enter the empty
and the nonempty.

Hey, fool! Can't you see
between those two,
empty and nonempty?

between those two: This phrase evokes the ontological "middle way," so often propounded by Buddhists (e.g., in the Madhyamaka philosophy of Nāgārjuna), between eternalism and nihilism, or the assertion that phenomena exist absolutely and immutably and the assertion that they do not exist at all.

12

sahaja ekku para atthi tahi phuḍa kāṇhu parijāṇai
satthāgama vahu paḍhai suṇai vaḍha kimpi ṇa jāṇai

The innate above all
is one—Kāṇha understands it
clearly and well;

fools recite
so many treatises and scriptures,
and know nothing at all.

13

aha ṇa gamai ūha ṇa jāi
veṇi-rahia tasu niccala ṭhai
bhaṇai kāṇha maṇa kahavi ṇa phuṭṭhai
ṇi[c]cala pavaṇa ghariṇi ghare vaṭṭai

It doesn't move up,
it doesn't go down;

doing neither, it stops there,
motionless.

Kāṇha says: thought
can't possibly escape

when motionless breath,
the mistress, remains at home.

the mistress: Literally, the "female householder." Thought, implicitly, is the male householder, who cannot leave the house (i.e., the central channel of the subtle body) as long as his female counterpart, the breath, remains inside it.

14

varagiri-kandara guhira jagu tahi saala vi tuṭṭai
vimala salila sosa jāi jai kālāgni paiṭṭhai

The precious mountain cave
is deep—the whole world
is sundered there;

stainless waters
dry up, until
the fire of time ignites.

mountain cave: A symbol of the central channel of the subtle body, which itself is likened to a great mountain, such as Meru, seen in many Indian mythologies as the center of the world. ***stainless water:*** Perhaps a reference to the stilling of the innate blissful, empty gnosis, or awakening mind, which is stainless by nature. ***fire of time:*** The *kālāgni* is an apocalyptic event on a macrocosmic scale, but here, given the yogic nature of Kāṇha's references, most likely connotes an individual's enlightenment, the final event in his or her career as a sentient being.

15

ehu so ūddhameru dharaṇidhara sama visama uttāra ṇa pāvai
bhāṇai kāṇha dullakkha duravahāha ko maṇe paribhāvai

Lofty Meru, support of the world,
is uncertain terrain—
you won't reach the top;

Kanha says: it's barely visible,
hard to approach—
who can encompass it with mind?

Meru: As noted, the mythic mountain at the center of the world, here a symbol for the subtle body, "barely visible, hard to approach" except for those with proper initiation and yogic prowess. Its top, where resides the innate, blissful, inmost mind, is difficult to scale, for the yogic practices that give one access to it are the most arduous a human being can undertake.

16

jo saṃveai maṇa raaṇa aharaha sahaja pharanta
so paru jāṇai dhamma-gai aṇṇa ki muṇai kahanta

If daily you discern
the thought jewel,
the innate shining forth,

you know how things really go—
others talk of it,
but what do they know?

thought jewel: A synonym for the awakening mind, or bodhicitta, which in the tantric context is identified with the blissful drop residing at the crown cakra. See K3.

17

pahaṃ vahante ṇia-maṇa vandhaṇa kiau jeṇa
tihuaṇa saala viphāriā puṇu saṃhāria teṇa

As you travel the path,
if you manage to bind
your inmost thought,

you'll emit
the whole triple world,
then draw it back again.

you'll emit the whole triple world: A reference to the extraordinary creative powers of thought once it has been brought under control. In fact, whether or not one controls one's inmost thought, that is, the innate gnosis, it is there that the world rises and falls. Tantra, however, gives one the tools to control that process: in generation-stage yogas, one visualizes emitting and reabsorbing the world in divinized form; in the completion-stage yogas that are Kāṇha's primary referent, one actually learns to transform cosmic processes, at least as they relate to oneself—though the lore of the Indian great adepts (mahāsiddhas), among whom Kāṇha is counted, suggests that the powers one gains through tantra may be exercised on a "public" scale in addition to the private one.

18

kāhiṃ tathāgata labhae devī koha-gaṇahi
maṇḍala-cakka-vimukka acchauṃ sahaja-khaṇehi

How is the Thus-Gone gained?
In the company
of wrathful goddesses;

free from the maṇḍala circle,
I live in
the innate moment.

Thus-Gone: One of the commonest epithets of a Buddha, *tathāgata*. It sometimes glossed as the One Thus Come (*tathā āgata*), sometimes as One Thus Gone (*tathā gata*), and sometimes as One Gone to and/or returned from Thusness (*tatha[tā] gata*); for the latter interpretation, see HT 1:5, 8. ***wrathful goddesses:*** The various female deities that are particularly featured in the Yoginī tantras practiced by Kāṇha; see, for example, HT 1: 8, 10–20, ST 13:22–27. Such spiritually efficacious beings as yoginīs and ḍākinīs may be understood as symbolic, as visualized, as manifest in concrete females—or all of these. ***free from the maṇḍala circle:*** Perhaps an indication that Kāṇha has moved beyond the visualization-centered practices of the generation stage to the transformative subtle body practices of the completion stage. The compound is ambiguous, though; it also may be read as indicating that Kāṇha is free in or through the maṇḍala circle. This would tally better with apparent meaning of K9. ***the innate moment:*** As for Saraha, the moment at which one attains innate ecstasy, the highest of the four successive ecstatic experiences induced in the central channel of the subtle body.

19

sahaje ṇiccala jeṇa kia samarasem ṇiamaṇa-rāa
siddho so puṇa takkhaṇe ṇau jarāmaraṇaha bhāa

When you're motionless in the innate,
to your inmost royal mind
things taste the same;

there's perfection in that moment,
and no more fear
of aging or death.

20

ṇiccala ṇivviappa ṇivviāra
uaa-atthamaṇa-rahia susāra
aiso so ṇivvāṇa bhaṇijjai
jahiṃ maṇa māṇasa kimpi ṇa kijjai

Motionless, nonconceptual,
changeless,

beyond rising or setting,
good to the core—

that's how we speak of nirvāṇa,
where thought

has nothing to do
with thinking.

21

evaṃkāra je vujjhia te vujjhia saala asesa
dhamma-karaṇḍaho sohu re ṇia-pahudhara-vesa

Awaken to Evaṃkāra,
and you awaken
to everything there is;

that alone contains what is—
hey, it's the dwelling of
your inmost potentate.

what is: My translation here for the untranslatable *dhamma* (Skt. *dharma*). On this term, see, for example, the note to S3.

22

jai pavaṇa-gamaṇa-duāre diḍha tālā vi dijjai
jai tasu ghorāndāreṃ maṇa divaho kijjai
jiṇa-raaṇa uareṃ jai so varu amvaru chuppai
bhaṇai kāṇha bhava muñjante nivvāṇo vi sijjhai

If the door
where the breath goes out
is fastened tight,

if thought is made a lamp
in the awful darkness there,

if the precious gem of the Victor
touches the top of the sky,

then, says Kāṇha,
delighting in existence,
you'll still perfect nirvāṇa.

gem: Again, the "thought jewel," or blissful awakening mind, which is located at the top of the subtle body, and includes the realization of emptiness, often symbolized by the sky. ***the Victor:*** The *jina*, another common epithet for a Buddha, seen as one who has gained victory over the forces of the Evil One, Māra, a symbol for saṃsāra itself.

23

jo ṇatthu ṇiccala kiau maṇa so dhammakkhara pāsa
pavaṇaho vajjhai takkhaṇe visaā honti ṇirāsa

When a master
makes thought motionless
by the syllable of truth

and binds the breath as well—
in that moment,
things are unhoped for.

syllable of truth: As in the case of Saraha's "single syllable" (S90) this may be the "unstruck sound" (Skt. *anāhata*) that is the source of all audible sounds, hence, symbolically, emptiness (the true nature of things). Realization of emptiness in the context of stilling one's breath is productive of a state beyond ordinary desires or wishes yet replete with bliss. ***unhoped for:*** That is, no longer subject to delusive fantasies of wish fulfillment; paradoxically, when such a state is attained, one truly is in the position of being able to fulfill all wishes.

24

parama virama jahiṃ veṇṇi uekkhai
tahiṃ dhammakkhara majjhe lakkhai
aisa uese jai phuḍa sijjhai
pavaṇa ghariṇi tahi ṇiccala vajjhai

Where zenith and nadir
both are unseen,

there in the middle,
the syllable of truth is perceived.

If you perfect clarity
by a teaching such as this,

the mistress, breath,
is bound there, motionless.

zenith and nadir: *Parama* and *virama* both have a considerable range of meanings, from high and low points, to pleasure and displeasure, to—in a Yoginī tantra context—the utmost ecstasy and the ecstasy of cessation. On the most general level, Kāṇha seems to be indicating that where truth is attained, and emptiness realized, dualities are overcome. In a specifically yogic context, it may indicate the transcendence of the utmost ecstasy and the ecstasy of cessation through the achievement of the innate ecstasy. See T26.

25

vara-giri-sihara utuṅga muṇi savareṃ jahiṃ kia vāsa
ṇau so laṃghia pañcāṇaṇehi karivara duria āsa

The lofty summit
of the precious peak,
where the mountain man makes his home,

is unconquered
by the five-faced fiend
and beyond the great elephant's hopes.

five-faced fiend: On a general level, this could refer to Śiva, or to the five defilements that hinder us on the spiritual path (desire, anger, ignorance, pride, envy); in the context of yogic practice, it may connote the five vital energies that course through the subtle body (upward, downward, vitalizing, pervasive, equalizing) and that must be "overcome" when energies are drawn into the central channel. ***great elephant:*** Here, probably, a symbol for the restless, conceptual mind, which, like the five energies, must be overcome in yogic practice within the central channel. For other uses of this image, see S100–101.

26

ehu so girivara kahia maiṃ ehuso mahāsuha-ṭhāva
ekku raaṇi sahaja khaṇa la[b]bhai mahāsuha jāva

It's the precious mountain, I say—
it alone is the place
of great bliss;

in a single night,
the innate moment is gained,
and great bliss descends.

a single night: This reference highlights the "nocturnal" aspect of tantric practices, some of which originated in late-night rituals in cremation grounds. It also suggests the darkness of emptiness that must come over the mind if truth is to be realized. Finally, the reference to a *single* night suggests the speed with which the tantric path may be traversed; through it, one may attain Buddhahood in this very life. ***great bliss descends:*** A reference to the "melting" of the male drop at the crown of the head through its activation by inner energies, and its subsequent descent through the central channel of the subtle body, with its attendant experience of the various ecstasies. It is a process occurring naturally on the occasion of ordinary sexual intercourse and in a controlled manner during completion-stage practices in the Yoginī and other advanced tantras.

27

sava jagu kāa-vāa-maṇa mili viphurai tahiso dure
so ehu bhaṅge mahāsuha ṇivvāṇa ekku re

The whole world—
this mix of body, speech, and thought—
is sundered there;

in this rupture,
great bliss and nirvāṇa—
hey, they're one!

there: A reference to the precious mountain, which in turn is a symbol for the central channel of the subtle body.

28

ekku ṇa kijjai manta ṇa tanta
ṇia ghariṇi lai keli karanta
ṇia ghare ghariṇi jāva ṇa majjai
tāva ki pañcavaṇṇa viharijjai

Mantras don't do a thing,
and neither do tantras:

embrace your inmost mistress,
and indulge in play.

Until the mistress descends
to her inmost home,

why not entertain
the five senses?

inmost mistress: The "mistress" is, as earlier (K13), the breath and its related energies; oneself is the mind. When these are under strict control one is, paradoxically, free to indulge the senses, without fear of attachment. The mistress here also may be the female personification of wisdom, regarded as a visualized goddess or yoginī ("gnosis seal": jñānamudrā), with whom, like the senses, one may engage until she reaches her "inmost home," the fruit of nondual blissful, empty gnosis, or enlightenment (the "great seal": mahāmudrā). For discussions of the "seals," see, for example, HT 2:4.

29

eso japa-home maṇḍala-kamme
aṇudiṇa acchasi kāhiu dhamme
to viṇu taruṇi ṇirantara ṇeheṃ
vohi ki la[b]bhai eṇa vi deheṃ

These chants, oblations,
and maṇḍala rites:

what worth is there
in such everyday acts?

O maiden,
without your ceaseless passion,

how will I gain awakening
in this body?

maiden: Another "feminine" reference, with a typical range of possible meanings, from an "action seal" (Skt. *karmamudrā*), with whom one practices sexual yoga, to a symbol of the blissful, empty gnosis that is the inmost nature of ourselves and the world.

30

jeṃ vujjhia virala sahajakhaṇa kāhiṃ vea-purāṇa
teṃ tuḍia visaa-viappa jagu re asesa parimāṇa

When you comprehend
that rare innate moment,
what need for Vedas or Purāṇas?

Your concepts of things are shattered.
Hey! You know the world
in every detail.

Your concepts . . . every detail: As earlier, in S63, it is paradoxically asserted that in the innate gnosis, all conceptuality is destroyed, yet one knows the world, as a Buddha does, in every detail, like a perfectly reflective mirror.

31

jeṃ kia ṇiccala maṇa-raaṇa ṇia ghariṇi lai ettha
soha vājira ṇāhu re mayiṃ vutto paramattha

Immobilize your thought jewel,
embrace your inmost mistress
in this very place—

and you'll be
a vajra-bearing master.
Hey! I sing the ultimate.

vajra-bearing master: The *vajra*, which may be translated as "scepter," thunderbolt," or "diamond," is a symbol of the indestructibility and impermeability of the enlightened state; in tantra, an enlightened being is said to have attained a vajra body, speech, and mind, and attained the status of being a vajra holder, Vajradhāra, a personification of the tantrically enlightened master.

32

jima loṇa vilijjai pāṇiehi tima ghariṇi lai citta
samarasa jāi takkhaṇe jai puṇu te sama ṇitta

Like salt dissolved in water
is mind
in the mistress's embrace;

they taste the same
in that moment,
and they'll be the same forever.

salt dissolved in water: The reference here is to the inseparability of gnosis and great bliss. For another, similar, evocation of salt in water, see S78b.

Tilopa's *Treasury of Couplets*

1

kandha [bhūa] āattaṇa indī
sahajasahāveṃ saala vivindī

Aggregates, elements,
fields and the senses—

all are bound up
in your innate nature.

Aggregates . . . senses: See the note to S92.

2

sahajeṃ bhāvābhāva ṇa pucchaha
suṇṇakaruṇ[ā] tahi samarasa icchaha

In the innate, don't ask
for existence or for nothingness—

seek there emptiness and compassion,
which taste the same.

taste the same: As before (e.g., S42e), the use of *samarasa* indicates that there is, in the final analysis, that is, in the innate, no distinction between the two major elements of the Mahāyāna path, cultivation of compassion (which is an antidote to the nihilistic quest for nothingness) and realization of emptiness (which is an antidote to attachment to saṃsāric existence).

3

māraha citta ṇivvāṇeṃ haṇiā
tihuaṇasuṇṇaniranjaṇa pasiā

Mind must be killed!
Destroy it with nirvāṇa,

and enter the undefiled emptiness
of the triple world.

[Tor 4]

4

amaṇasiāra ma dūsaha micche
appaṇuvandha ma karahu re icche

Don't disparage unthinking
with your falsehood—

Hey! Don't seek
to put yourself in bondage.

[Tor 3]

unthinking: A reference to the meditative procedure wherein, as part of the process of moving beyond conceptual thought, one "does not bring anything to mind" (Skt. *amanasikāra*). This procedure came to be especially associated with the eleventh-century Indian master Maitrīpa, who is credited in Tibetan accounts with writing "Twenty-Five Texts on Unthinking"; these texts, in turn, were influential in a number of Tibetan practice lineages, most notably the Kagyu, for whom Saraha and Tilopa also are crucial figures.

5

citta khasama jahi samasuha paiṭṭhai
[indīa-visaa tahi matta] ṇa dīsai

When spacious mind
joins with the bliss of sameness,

then senses and their objects
no longer appear.

sameness: See the note to S42b, to which this verse bears some resemblance.

6

āirahia ehu antarahia
varagurupāa a[ddaa kahia]

It's without a beginning,
without an end—

at the precious guru's feet
is the nondual declared

7

tu maraj jahi pavaṇa tahi līṇo hoi ṇirāsa
saa [saṃveaṇa tattaphalu] sa kahijjai kīsa

Where mind
has died, breath
is completely dissolved;

the self-aware
fruit of the real:
to whom can it be told?

8

vaḍa aṇaṃloa-agoara-tatta paṇḍialoa-agamma
jo gurupā[apasaṇṇa tahiṃ ki citta agamma]

Fool! The real
eludes regular folks,
and scholars can't approach it,

but if you're blessed
at the guru's feet,
how can mind not approach it?

how can mind not approach it? The message here is set, both stylistically and semantically, in contrast to the last line of T8 (and to some degree, T9–9a). There, the ineffability and incommunicability of reality is stressed; here, its comprehensibility to anyone blessed by the guru is asserted. Once again, the statements are paradoxical without being contradictory, for ordinary conceptualization never can capture the ultimate, but symbolically charged discourse communicated by a guru can bring the ineffable within the range of a disciple's understanding, though the understanding is of a gnostic variety.

9

saasaṃveaṇa tattaphala tīlapāa bhaṇanti
[jo maṇagoara paiṭhṭhai so paramattha ṇa honti]

Self-awareness,
fruit of the real—
Tilopāda's saying:

what falls within
the range of thought
is not the ultimate.

9a

de nyid bla ma'i gsung gis bstan par bya ba min
des na slob mas go ba ma yin no
lhan skyes 'bras bu bdud rtsi'i ro
de nyid su zhig la ni ci zhig bstan

The real
can't be shown
by the guru's words,

so the disciple
cannot comprehend.

The fruit of the innate
tastes ambrosial;

who teaches the real
to whom?

[no B, *Tor 10a–d*]

The real. . . . whom? The similarity in language and meaning between this and S56a suggests that they may represent two different Tibetan translations of the same Apabhraṃśa original, though whether it originally belonged to "Saraha" or "Tilopa," we cannot say.

9b

gang du yid ni zhi ba dang
yid dang rlung gnyis mnyam par zhu
der ni rnam kun spangs pa la
khams gsum de ru gnas pa yin

When thought is pacified
and thought and breath
melt into sameness,

every detail is rejected there—
there the triple world
has come to rest.

[no B, *Tor 10e–h*]

9c

rmongs pa gnyug ma'i rang bzhin shes par gyis
de tshe gti mug dra ba ma lus chad par 'gyur

Fool! You must know
your inmost nature—

then you'll cut the net
of ignorance, every strand.

[no B, *Tor 10i–j*]

10

sahajeṃ citta visohahu caṅga
iha jammahi siddhi [mokkha bhaṅga]

In the innate:
purify well the mind;

in this very life:
perfection, freedom, release.

[Tor 11]

11

jahi jāi citta tahi suṇahu acitta
samarasaṃ [ṇimmala bhāvābhāvarahia]

Where mind
has disappeared to, listen:
there's the nonmind, too;

they taste the same:
they're stainless, beyond
existence and nothingness.

[Tor 12]

11a

tshe 'di nyid la dngos grub legs par gsal por rnyed
sems ni gang du zhi gyur pa
khams gsum po ni de ru thim

In this very life,
clearly and well
you'll gain perfection;

where mind is becalmed,
the triple world dissolves.

[no B, *Tor 13a–c*]

11b

rang gzhan mnyam pas sangs rgyas rje btsun 'gyur
sems ni nam mkha'i ngang du zhugs nas thim
de tshe'i dbang po lnga dang yul rnams dang
phung po khams rnams nang du zhugs nas song

When self and other are the same,
you become a holy Buddha;

mind enters the realm of space,
and dissolves.

Then the five senses
and their objects,

the aggregates and elements,
enter within, and are gone.

[no B, *Tor 13*]

mind enters . . . are gone: The process described here is the progressive, yogically controlled "dissolution" or absorption of various mental and physical faculties. This controlled process mimics, anticipates, and ultimately helps one to control the same processes that occur in an uncontrolled manner at the time of death. In this sense, advanced tantric practices involve a systematic preenactment of one's own death, so that death may be overcome.

12

addaa cittataruara gau tihuaṇa vitthāra
karuṇā-phulia-phala-dhara ṇau parata uāra

The precious tree
of nondual mind
spreads through the triple world;

it bears compassion flower and fruit,
though there is no other
or doing good.

[no Tor]

The precious . . . good: This verse is identical to S107. Its absence from Tibetan translations of Tilopa's *Dohākoṣa* probably indicates that later redactors and translators regarded it as Saraha's, though it is common for Indian authors to appropriate sayings from one another without attribution.

13

para appāṇa ma bhanti karu saala nirantara vuddha
tihuaṇa ṇimmala paramapau citta sahāveṃ suddha

Don't be confused
about other and self—
all are unceasingly Buddha;

the triple world:
the stainless, utmost place,
mind quite naturally pure.

[no Tor]

Don't . . . . pure: This verse, too, is missing from the Tibetan. It is nearly identical to S106, the only difference coming at the beginning of the second line, where "Saraha" has *ehu se* ("that's it") in place of "Tilopa's" *tihuaṇa* ("the triple world"). As with T12, its absence from the Tibetan indicates that later redactors attributed it to Saraha.

14

sacala ṇicala jo saalācara
suṇa nirañjaṇa ma karu viāra

Every aspect,
moving or motionless,

is empty and unadorned—
don't analyze!

15

ehuse appā ehu jagu jo paribhāvai
[ṇimmala cittasahāva so ki vujjhai]

If you think, "this is the self,"
"this is the cosmos,"

how will you waken to mind
that's naturally stainless?

"this . . . cosmos": Compare this fairly traditional Buddhist formulation of the absence of self with T16 and T 34.

16

haṃu jagu haṃu vuddha haṃu nirañjaṇa
[haṃu amaṇasiāra bhavabhañjaṇa]

I am the cosmos, I am the Buddha,
I am the unadorned,

I am unthinking—
I've broken existence!

I am . . . . : Compare the positive rhetoric here (reminiscent of that found in many Hindu texts, but in Buddhist tantras, as well: see, e.g., HT 1:8, 37; 1:8, 39; 2:2, 37) with the more skeptical approach in T15 and the more negative formulation in T34. In combination, the two expressions may indicate that I am the cosmos (etc.) in the sense that I, like the cosmos, have the ultimate nature of being empty. I have shown, though, that emptiness may not be inalterably negative in its connotations for tāntrikas, so there may be quasi-substantialist implications of this verse that even the negations of T34 cannot erase.

17

maṇaha [bhaavā] khasama bhaavai
[divārātti sahaje rāhiai]

Thought is the lord,
spaciousness the lady:

day and night they're joined
in the innate.

Thought . . . lady: Another instance of the polar gender symbolism so common in tantric traditions, here applied to the "coupling" of mind and space, or consciousness and emptiness, which, in the experience of the innate, are inseparable. See, for example, S42a.

◎ 18

jammamaraṇa mā karahu re bhanti
[ṇiacitta tahiṃ ṇirantara honti]

Hey! Don't get confused
about birth and death;

and your inmost mind
exists there, unceasing.

exists there, unceasing: The "there" (Apa. *tahiṃ,* Skt. *tatra*) is ambiguous, but the implication seems to be that the inmost mind, i.e., the innate, is to be found in the midst of birth and death. The Tibetan of the second line (whose Apabhraṃśa has been restored by Bagchi) is a command to dwell unceasingly in the inmost mind (*gnyug ma'i yid la rgyun du gnas par gyis*).

◎ 19

tittha-tapovaṇa ma karahu sevā
[dehasucihi ṇa sānti pāvā]

Don't visit pilgrim spots
or hermitages:

you won't gain peace
through cleansing the body.

Don't . . . body: See S15.

◎ 20

vamhā vihṇu mahesura devā
[vohisattva ma karahu sevā]

Brahmā, Viṣṇu, Śiva:
these are gods,

O bodhisattva,
you should not serve.

bodhisattva: This is the only explicit reference in any of these three *Dohākoṣas* to the ideal figure of the Mahāyāna, the bodhisattva, who seeks to perfect skillful methods and deep-seeing wisdom in order to attain full Buddhahood for the sake of all sentient beings. The trio of Brahmā, Viṣṇu, and Śiva are regarded by Buddhists as being merely worldly deities, unworthy as objects of refuge.

◎ 21

deva ma pūjahu ti[ttha ṇa jāvā
devapūjāhi ṇa mokkha pāvā]

Don't worship gods!
Don't go on pilgrimage!

Worshipping gods,
you won't reach freedom.

22

vuddha ārahāhu avikalacitteṃ
[bhavaṇivvāṇe ma karahu re thitteṃ]

Honor Buddha
by nonconceptual mind;

Hey! Don't get stuck in existence—
or nirvāṇa.

23

paggopāa-samāhi laggahu jahi
tahi diḍha kara aṇuttara siddhai

Fixed in the union
of wisdom and method,

surely you'll perfect
the unsurpassed.

the union of wisdom and method: One of the paramount concepts of Mahāyāna and tantric Buddhism, representing the combination of characteristics possessed by a Buddha. On the Mahāyāna plane, it refers primarily to the conjunction of insight into emptiness with compassionate methods for liberating others. In a Yoginī tantra context, it refers, among many other things, to the inseparability of the realization of emptiness and the experience of great bliss in the innate gnosis that is the original nature of mind. It also may refer to the two partners in sexual yoga practices.

24

jima visa bhakkhai visahi paluttā
[tima bhava bhuñjai bhavahi ṇa juttā]

Like a poison expert
partaking of poison,

delight in existence
but don't get hooked on existence.

poison expert partaking of poison: One of the commonest images used by tantric authors to illustrate how tantric practice allows one to partake of the forbidden—as long as one has sufficient discipline and detachment not to be affected by it; see, for example, HT 2:2, 46.

25

kamma mudda ma dūsaha joi
[khaṇa āṇanda bheu jāṇijjai]

Yogin! Don't disparage
the physical woman—

through her, you'll know
what moments and ecstasies are.

physical woman: Literally, the "action seal" (Skt. *karmamudrā*), a flesh-and-blood consort with whom certain highly advanced yogins engage in sexual yoga practices, so as to move vital energies and drops through the central channel of the subtle body, thereby inducing the four momentary ecstasies (ecstasy, utmost ecstasy, ecstasy of cessation, and innate ecstasy) that are so important to success in the Yoginī tantras.

26

lahu re parama virama viāri
ṇiuṇeṃ varaguru-caraṇa ārāhi

Hey! Reflecting on the utmost
and on cessation,

approach devoutly
the feet of the precious guru.

utmost and . . . cessation: In a fourfold system, the two "middle" ecstasies induced by the movement of energies and drops within the central channel. As earlier (K24), the terms also may be taken more generally, as zenith and nadir, or any pair of apparent opposites, but I have chosen the more technical translations here because in verses 25–28, Tilopa seems to be describing a sequence of experiences related to the four ecstasies.

27

[parama āṇanda bheu jo jāṇai
khaṇahi sovi sahaja vujjhai]

When you know just what
utmost ecstasy is,

at that very moment,
you'll waken to the innate.

27a

yon tan rin chen dpral ba'i klad rgyas gzhag bya ste
'dod pa mo yi ze 'bru las ni 'di [nyid] shes par bya

Set and seal the invaluable gem
at the crown of the head!

Do this through
a passionate woman's embrace.

[no B, *Tor 28*]

Do: The Tibetan verb actually is shes par bya, "know," but I believe that here it carries the sense of "do," or "effect," for it is through (Tib. *las*) the embrace—i.e., sexual yoga—that one induces the experiences that culminate in the stabilization of the "gem" (the white drop, or awakening mind at the crown cakra) in the experience of innate ecstasy.

28

khaṇa āṇanda bheu jo jāṇai
so iha jammahi joi bhaṇijjai

When you know just what
the moments and ecstasies are,

you'll be proclaimed a yogin
in this very life.

[Tor 29]

moments and ecstasies: See the note to S95.

28a

thog ma tha ma gzung ba 'dzin pa spangs
bla ma mchog gi zhabs kyis gnyis med bstan
mi g.yo dri med rnam par rtog pa med
shar ba nub pa spangs pa 'di ni snying po yin
'di ni mya ngan 'das par rab tu brjod
yid kyi nga rgyal gang du chad gyur pa

Give up beginning and end,
object and subject:

the nondual is taught
at the precious guru's feet.

Motionless, stainless,
nonconceptual, too,

beyond rise and fall—
this is the heart of it.

This, it's clearly proclaimed,
is nirvāṇa,

where all prideful thought
is cut off.

[no B, *Tor 30*]

Give up . . . : This and the following, final verses of Tilopa's text are a general description of the innate, recapitulating many of the themes that he, and the other two poets, have expounded before.

29

guṇadosa-rahia ehu paramattha
saasaṃveaṇeṃ kevi ṇatha

What's beyond both virtues and flaws
is the ultimate;

in self-awareness,
there is no thing at all.

[Tor 31]

beyond both virtues and flaws: See S38.

30

cittācitta vivajjahu ṇitta
sahajasarūeṃ karahu re thitta

Give up mind
and nonmind forever more.

Hey! Make your abode
in the uniform innate.

[Tor 32]

31

skye ba med cing 'chi ba med
rtsa ba med cing rtse mo med
āvai jāi kahavi ṇa ṇai
guruuvaeseṃ hiahi samāi

It isn't born,
it doesn't die,
it has no root or top;

"it comes" and "it goes"
do not apply—

but with the guru's teaching,
it enters the heart.

[*Tor 33* (first two lines)]

It . . .top: There is no Apabhraṃśa extant for the first two lines, and although the last two lines could stand on their own, I have added the material included in the Tibetan version of the verse, which does seem semantically relevant.

32

vaṇṇa vi vajjai ākii-vihuṇṇā
savvāāre so saṃpuṇṇā

It's drained of all color,
lacking a shape—

yet fulfilled
in every appearance.

[Tor 34]

33

e maṇa mārahu [lahu citte] ṇimmūla
[tahiṃ mahāmudda tihuaneṃ ṇimmala]

Quick! Kill the thought
that is not rooted in mind—

thus is the great seal:
stainless in the triple world.

[Tor 35]

thought not rooted in mind: This is one of the very few instances in which "thought" (*maṇa*) and "mind" (*citta*) appear in the same dohā, and in this case the priority is clear: mind is the more fundamental term (it seems to refer here to the innate gnosis), thought the more superficial (referring to conceptuality and intellectualization). ***great seal:*** *Mahāmudda* (Skt. *mahāmudrā*), a term used frequently in the Yoginī tantras to denote the final fruit of the tantric path, that is, Buddhahood, which is the experience of the blissful, empty gnosis that is the inmost nature of ourselves and the world; see, for example, HT 1:8, 41, 2: 4, 43, ST 3:16. Its "conventional" form is as a partner for sexual yoga practice; see, for example HT 2:8, 1–5. In other contexts, especially those of the "lower tantras," it may refer to a hand gesture used in tantric ritual or, simply, emptiness. And in later Indian, and Tibetan, traditions it comes to denote a style or technique of meditation in which the focus is on the true nature of the mind. It is especially important in the Kagyu order. See the note to K28.

34

hau suṇṇa jagu suṇṇa tihuaṇa suṇṇa
[ṇimmala sahaje ṇa pāpa ṇa puṇṇa]

I am empty, the cosmos empty,
the triple world empty, too;

in the stainless innate,
there is no vice or virtue.

[T 36]

I am . . . : See the notes to T15 and T16. ***virtue:*** See the note to K10.

35

jahi icchai tahi jāu maṇa etthu ṇa kijjai bhanti
adha ughāḍya āloaṇe jjhāṇe hoi re thitti

Let thought go
where it wishes—
it can't go wrong there;

now that my eyes
are open, I'll meditate.
Hey! I'm set.

[T 37]

meditation: Here, despite the many negative comments about meditation and contemplation, especially by Saraha, it is clear that meditation *is* a technique a tantric practitioner must learn—but it must be practiced correctly, without excessive restriction, without expectation, without conceptualization, without dualistic thought, without, finally, any distinction between meditating and not meditating. See S78a.

Notes

1. On the mahāsiddhas in general, see, e.g., Dasgupta 1976, Dowman 1985, Ray 1986, Davidson 2002a: chaps. 5–7, White 2003: chap. 6.

2. For translations of Abhayadattaśrī's text, see Robinson 1979, Dowman 1985. For material relating to songs sung by, and liturgies related to, the eighty-four, see Egyed 1984, Kapstein 2000.

3. On the eighty-five, see Schmid 1958; for the Nepalese guru list, see Tucci 1930; on the fifty-nine, see Templeman 1983; for Nyingma versions, see Dudjom 1991; on yoginīs, see Shaw 1994.

4. On Paśupatas and Kāpālikas, see Lorenzen 1972, Davidson 2002a: chap. 5; on Kashmiri Śaivites, see Mishra 1993, Sanderson 1988; on Bengali Śaktas, see Avalon 1974, McDaniel 1989; on the Nāth and Rasa siddhas, see White 1996; for Patañjali, see, for example, Radhakrishnan and Moore 1957: 453–485; on Saṃnyāsa Upaniṣads, see Olivelle 1992; on Nāgas, etc., see Bedi 1991.

5. Bharati 1970: chap. 1, especially 28–30.

6. For representative lists, see, for example, Robinson 1979: 289–307, Dudjom 1991: 2: 199–290.

7. On issues related to Saraha, see Shahidullah 1928: chap. 2, Y. Nara 1966, Guenther 1969: 3–20, Dowman 1985: 69–72, Guenther 1993: 3–15, R. Jackson 1994, 1996a, Schaeffer 2000 (especially chap. 8). For traditional biographies, see Robinson 1979: 41–43, Dowman 1985: 66–69, Templeman 1983: 2–3, Guenther 1993: 3–7. For translations of texts attributed to Saraha, see, e.g., Shahidullah 1928: 169–181, 233–234, Snellgrove 1954, Kvaerne 1977: 168–171, 199–202, 222–231, Guenther 1969: 63–71, Guenther 1993: 89–157, Cleary 1998: 111–112, 137–139, 161–169, Schaeffer 2000: 271–348. The *Dohākoṣa* translated here is, in the Tibetan setting, referred to as the "People" *Treasury of Couplets*, in contradistinction to the "Queen" and "King" collections; Guenther 1969 is translation and commentary on the *King Treasury of Couplets*, and Guenther 1993 includes translations of all three. Given his "foundational" role in various tantric lineages, especially that of the great seal, Saraha—if he lived at all—may have been the earliest of the three authors, but his dates cannot reasonably be narrowed beyond the general assertion that he probably lived some time between the eighth and eleventh centuries.

8. On issues related to Kāṇha, see Shahidullah 1928: 3–4, and chap. 2, Dowman 1985: 128–131, Templeman 1989: 107, R. Jackson 1992. For traditional biographies, see Robinson 1979: 81–85, Dowman 1985: 123–127, Templeman 1983: 43–44, Templeman 1989. For translations of texts attributed to Kāṇha under one or another of his names, see Shahidullah 1928: 85–88, 117–122, Beyer 1974: 258–261, Kvaerne 1977: 100–104, 109–135, 150–158, 214–218, 231–234, 238–241, 248–250, Farrow and Menon 1992, Cleary 1998: 41–43, 49–72, 97–103, 171–173, 179–181, 191–193. Like Saraha, Kāṇha is extremely difficult to date;

we have a bit more evidence to go on in his case, but much of it is conflicting, and the range of dates we might supply for him is, in the end, rather similar to Saraha's (sometime between the eighth and eleventh centuries); for a discussion, see Snellgrove 1959: 1:13, n. 4, Templeman 1989: 107, n. 3.

9. The six are the practices of inner heat, illusory body, clear light, dream, transference of consciousness, and the intermediate state; for discussions, see, for example, Chang 1963, Mullin 1996, Mullin 1997.

10. On issues related to Tilopa, see Dowman 1985: 151–155, Nālandā Translation Committee 1982: xxxi–xxxii, Torricelli 1997. For traditional biographies, see Robinson 1979: 98–99, Dowman 1985: 151, Templeman 1983: 45–46, Gyaltsen 1990: 33–54, Thrangu 1993: 5–42, Nālandā Translation Committee 1997, as well as Guenther 1963, where he is discussed in the context of his role as guru to Nāropa. For translations of texts attributed to Tilopa, see, for example, Chang 1963: 25–30, Bhattacharyya 1982: 289–291, Thaye 1990: 75–76, Bercholz and Kohn 1993: 266–272, Mullin 1997: 27–29. Tilopa is the only one of the three authors herein to whom precise dates sometimes are assigned: the most commonly given are 988–1069, but these may be too late, if we accept 1012–1097 as Marpa's dates and assume that Marpa was a disciple of Nāropa, and Nāropa of Tilopa.

11. This presumes—and most scholars do presume—that the dohās were, in fact, originally oral compositions; if they were not, they might well simply have been composed in Apabhraṃśa. On the language of the *Dohākoṣas*, see, for example, Shahidullah 1928: 53–55, Bagchi 1934, T. Nara 1961, T. Nara 1962, De 1993; on Apabhraṃśa, see, for example, Tagare 1987, Ghosal 1956, S. Sen 1973, Dimock et al. 1974: 12–13, Bubenik 1996.

12. On the dohā, see, e.g., Shahidullah 1928: chap. 4, N. Sen 1973, Schomer 1987, Templeman 1994: 17–26. The various metric patterns of the dohā are too complex to analyze here. For the beginnings of a discussion, see Shahidullah 1928: 60–62.

13. On performance songs and diamond songs, both in and of themselves and vis-à-vis dohās, see Templeman 1994. For examples of performance songs in translation, see Kvaerne 1977, Cleary 1998. For diamond songs, see, for example, HT 2: 4, 6–10, Templeman 1994: 26–29.

14. For examples of English translations of texts preserved only in Tibetan, see, e.g., Thaye 1990: 75–86, Kunga and Cutillo 1995: 26–27; for a discussion of related issues, see Schaeffer 2000: chap. 7.

15. For editions and translations of the *Hevajra*, see Snellgrove 1959, Farrow and Menon 1992; for the *Saṃvarodaya* (which is part of the Cakrasaṃvara tantra cycle), see Tsuda 1974; for the *Caṇḍamahārosana*, see George 1974; for the *Vajrakīlaya*, see Mayer 1996; for a discussion of aspects of the *Buddhakapāla* (on which Saraha apparently wrote a commentary), see Davidson 2002a: 247–252; for portions of the *Kālackra*, see Newman 1987; see also Wallace 2000.

16. Alternative names for Yoginī tantras include Prajñā (or wisdom) tantras and Ḍākinī tantras. Alternative names for Mahāyoga tantras include Upāya (method) tantras and Ḍāka tantras; see, for example, Lessing and Wayman 1978: 251.

17. As a number of scholars have pointed out, the usage of "tantra" as a generic term for a style of religious thought and praxis in India and beyond is to some degree an innovation of Western scholarship, which all too often has projected onto Asian traditions monolithic concepts that are not recognized by Asians themselves. As David White notes, an examination of the phenomena that scholars have called "tantra" reveals "a complex array of ritual, theoretical, and narrative strategies that are specific to their various religious, cultural,

sociopolitical, geographical and historical contexts." He adds, however, that "there nonetheless exists a grouping of common denominators that should permit us to classify these as so many varieties of a single tradition . . . of Tantra" (White 2000: 5). White then goes on to supply a definition, which (fortunately) he admits is subject to modification according to particular contexts: "Tantra is an Asian body of beliefs and practices which, working from the principle that the universe we experience is nothing other than the concrete manifestation of the divine energy of the godhead that creates and maintains the universe, seeks to ritually appropriate and channel that energy, within the human microscosm, in creative and emancipatory ways" (9).

18. On taxonomies of tantra, see, for example, Wayman 1973: 233–239, Tsong-ka-pa 1977, Thondup 1982, Snellgrove 1987: vol. 1, Karmay 1988: 146–151, Thondup 1989: 29–35, Dudjom 1991, K. Gyatso 1994.

19. On idiosyncracies of the Yoginī tantras, see, for example, Snellgrove 1987: 1:243–266, Williams 2000: 213–217, English 2002, Davidson 2002b; on Unsurpassed Yoga tantras, see K. Gyatso 1982, Cozort 1986, Snellgrove 1987: vol. 1, Newman, 2000; on Buddhist tantras in general, see Lessing and Wayman 1978, Snellgrove 1987: vol. 1, Dudjom 1991, Samuel 1993, K. Gyatso 1994, Sanderson 1994, Williams 2000: chap. 7; on Mahāyāna, see Williams 1989; on Buddhism in general, see Rahula 1974, Gethin 1998; on yoga as a pan-Indian movement, see Eliade 1969; on the relation between Buddhist and Hindu tantras, see Sanderson 1988, Sanderson 1994; on tantra in general, see Bharati 1970, White 2000, White 2003: chap. 1.

20. For an excellent summary of major themes in the dohās and caryāgīti, arranged somewhat differently, see Dasgupta 1976.

21. For the *Keṇa*, see, for example, Radhakrishnan and Moore 1957: 41; for the *Heart Sūtra*, see, for example, Conze 1958; for the *Lao Tzu*, see, for example, Chan 1963: 141; and for the *Gateless Gate*, see, for example, Shibayama 1974: cases 30 and 33.

22. Davidson (2002a) points out that "agonistic" rhetoric is especially prominent in Buddhist tantric literature, which was created against the background of competition by Buddhists and others for scarce sources of patronage in a fragmented medieval polity.

23. For translations as "the Innate," see, for example, Shahidullah 1928, Dasgupta 1976, and Snellgrove 1954; for "Together-born," see Lessing and Wayman 1978; for "Simultaneously-arisen," see Kvaerne 1975; for "the Spontaneous," see Beyer 1974; for "Coemergence" see Guenther 1969, Namgyal 1986; for "Connate," see Newman 2000; for "Complementarity-in-Spontaneity," see Guenther 1993, for "Being," see Torricelli 1997. Davidson (2002b) argues that the term must be translated according to its context. Still others (e.g., Urban 2001) simply leave the term untranslated. Snellgrove 1987: 1:245, n. 208, argues that "the innate" remains the best translation for *sahaja*, and I agree. Kvaerne 1975 and Davidson 2002b are the most cogent overall discussions of the term and its usages, though there also is much useful information in Shendge 1967 and Dasgupta 1976 (e.g., 77–86).

24. On the contrast between these views, see, for example, Ruegg 1963, Ruegg 1969, Williams 1989, Hookham 1991, Stearns 1999.

25. The siddhas' references to females (and their use of gender polarity symbolism) are significant and complex. The "actual" women to whom they refer in an apparently sexual manner may also, in other (e.g., monastic) contexts, merely be visualized partners, used to effect similar if not identical results. Women also may be taken as symbols of, for example, wisdom, or emptiness, or the blissful, empty gnosis of the innate, with whom the yogin "joins" (physically or not) to complete the classic Mahāyāna union of wisdom and method,

which is a prerequisite for Buddhahood. In other contexts, for example, as a house mistress, a woman may symbolize the breath, which must be "kept at home," or the unquiet mind, which mistakenly seeks its "husband," the true mind of the innate, in externals, rather than within. On the question the female as symbol and social being in Buddhist tantra, see, for example, Willis 1989, Shaw 1994, J. Gyatso 1998, Simmer-Brown 2001; on the question in Hindu tantra, see Kinsley 1997, White 2003.

26. For examples of this with relation to Saraha, see Guenther 1993 and Schaeffer 2000.

27. *Yoga Sūtra* 1.2; see, for example, Radhakrishnan and Moore 1957: 454, where the phrase is rendered: "*Yoga* is the restraint of mental modifications."

28. This sort of distinction is very important in Tibetan meditative systems influenced by the siddhas, such as the great perfection (Tib. *rdzogs chen*) of the Nyingma, where a clear line is drawn between ordinary mind (*sems*) and exalted, primordial mind (*rig pa*), and the great seal of the Kagyu, where a distinction sometimes is drawn between mind (*sems*) and mind itself (*sems nyid*). On the great perfection, see, for example, Karmay 1988, Thondup 1989, Norbu and Clemente 1999; on the great seal, see, for example, Gyaltsen 1983, Namgyal 1986, Martin 1992, D. Jackson 1994.

29. On these, see, for example, Snellgrove 1987: vol. 1.: 213–277.

30. See the accounts of Yoginī tantra ecstasy practice found in, for example, Chan 1963, Shendge 1967, K. Gyatso 1982, Snellgrove 1987: vol. 1, K. Gyatso 1991, Mullin 1996, and Mullin 1997, and the descriptions and analyses in Kvaerne 1975, Dasgupta 1976, and Davidson 2002b.

31. On this question, see, for example, Snellgrove 1987: vol. 1, R. Jackson 1992.

32. Two classic, early sources for understanding the two stages are ST chaps. 2–3, HT 1:8, 23; see also, for example, Beyer 1973, Gyaltsen 1983, Cozort 1986, Thurman 1995: chaps. 7–8. Beyer 1973 remains the most thorough and stimulating discussion of these two stages, which he designates the "Process of Generation" and the "Process of Perfection."

33. For Milarepa's story, see Lhalungpa 1986; for Saraha, Kāṇha, and Tilopa, see notes 7–8, 10.

34. For Kabīr, Ravidās, and Nānak, see Hawley and Jurgensmeyer 1988; for Jñānadeva, see Pradhan 1967; for Tukaram, see Chitre 1991; for Sultan Bahu, see Elias 1998; for Lallā, see Barks 1992; for Chandidās and Vidyāpati, see Dimock and Levertov 1967; on the Bāuls, see McDaniel 1989: chap. 4; on the Kartābhajās, see Urban 2001.

35. On Newar religion, see, for example, Gellner 1992, Lewis 2000.

36. On songs of experience, see R. Jackson 1996b; for Milarepa, see, for example, Chang 1989, Kunga and Cutillo 1995; for translations of a range of songs of experience from the premodern era, including those of several figures listed here, see Nālandā Translation Committee 1980, Jinpa and Elsner 2000; for modern figures, see, for example, Rabten 1983, Trungpa 1983.

37. For examples of Beat poetry linked to Buddhist themes, see Tonkinson 1995.

38. No. 124, Hess and Singh 1983: 104.

39. No. 12, Hess and Singh 1983: 91.

40. Nos. 6, 35, Hess and Singh 1983: 90, 93.

41. Nos. 96, 189, 160, Hess and Singh 1983: 100, 112, 107–108.

42. No. 348, Hess and Singh 1983: 130.

43. From "Poems and Fragments," Hillyer 1941: 586–587.

44. From "The Marriage of Heaven and Hell" ("The Voice of the Devil"), Hillyer 1941: 651–652.

45. Ibid. ("The Argument"), Hillyer 1941: 651.

46. Ibid. ("Proverbs of Hell"), Hillyer 1941: 654.

47. From "Poems and Fragments," Hillyer 1941: 575.

48. "The Question Answer'd," Hillyer 1941: 579.

49. From "There is no Natural Religion," Hillyer 1941: 619–620.

50. From "The Marriage of Heaven and Hell," Hillyer 1941: 657. The phrase "doors of perception" was taken by Aldous Huxley as the title of his book on mescaline and mysticism, and "the doors" was adopted by Jim Morrison for the name of his late-1960s rock group. In the Doors' song "End of the Night," Morrison directly quotes Blake's "Auguries of Innocence": "Some are Born to Sweet Delight, / Some are Born to Endless Night."

51. Hillyer 1941: 597.

52. Hillyer 1941: 597, 598.

53. Hillyer 1941: 599.

54. Hillyer 1941: 600.

55. Hillyer 1941: 598.

56. For different Apabhraṃśa versions of Saraha, see Śāstri 1916, Shahidullah 1928, Bagchi 1935, Bagchi 1938, Saṃkṛtyāyayana 1957; for the Tibetan, see Shahidullah 1928, Schaeffer 2000, and the recensions in, for example, the Derge (Tohoku no. 2224, Barber 1991: vol. 28) and Peking (Peking no. 3068, Suzuki 1957: vol. 68) editions of the Tibetan Tripiṭaka. For a concordance of verses among the editions of Śāstri, Bagchi, and Saṃkṛtyāyayana, see Saṃkṛtyāyayana 1957: 459–467. For the Apabhraṃśa of Kāṇha, see Shahidullah 1928, Bagchi 1935, Bagchi 1938; for the Tibetan, see Shahidullah 1928, as well as Barber 1991: vol. 28 (Tohoku no. 2301), Suzuki 1957: vol. 69 (Peking no. 3150). For the Apabhraṃśa of Tilopa, see Bagchi 1935, Bagchi 1938; for the Tibetan, see Torricelli 1997, as well as Barber 1991: vol. 28 (Tohoku no. 2281), Suzuki 1957: vol. 69 (Peking no. 3128).

57. See Schaeffer 2000: 220–230 for a clear discussion of some of these issues.

58. Some points worth noting with regard to pronunciation: (1) long vowels—indicated by a macron—receive greater stress than short ones, (2) in words of three or more syllables where no vowel is long, the stress is often on the third-to-last syllable (e.g., Niccala), (3) compound vowels are probably best pronounced if each component of the compound is separately articulated (e.g., paḍhi-a-u), and (4) many of the consonants transliterated as a "v" (e.g., in *vuddha*) may have been pronounced as a "b"—indeed, in Shahidullah's edition, b is generally used in preference to v, perhaps reflecting tendencies in Bengali, Apabhraṃśa's modern descendant.

59. Readers interested in such commentarial expansions may consult the Sanskrit commentaries to each provided by Bagchi. For Saraha, see also Guenther 1993 (especially the notes, in which he draws on a range of Indian and Tibetan commentaries) and Schaeffer 2000: 264–348 (which is a translation the commentary by the Tibetan scholar bCom ldan ral gri); for Tilopa, see Torricelli 1997.

Bibliography

Apte, Vaman Shivaram. [1965] 1998. *The Practical Sanskrit-English Dictionary*. Rev. and enl. ed. Delhi: Motilal Banarsidass.

Avalon, Arthur. [1919] 1974. *The Serpent Power: The Secrets of Tantric and Shaktic Yoga*. New York: Dover.

Bagchi, Prabodh Chandra. 1934. A Note on the Language of the Buddhist *Dohās*. *Calcutta Oriental Journal* 1, 7: 249–251.

———. 1935. Dohākoṣa with Notes and Translations. *Journal of the Department of Letters* [University of Calcutta] 28: 1–180.

———, ed. 1938. *Dohākoṣa: Apabhraṃśa Texts of the Sahajayāna School*. Calcutta Sanskrit series no. 25C. Calcutta: Metropolitan.

Barber, A. W., ed. 1991. *The Tibetan Tripiṭaka, Taipei Edition*. Taipei: SMC.

Barks, Coleman, trans. 1992. *Lalla: Naked Song*. Athens, Ga.: Maypop Books.

Bedi, Rajesh. 1991. *Sadhus, The Holy Men of India*. Text by Ramesh Bedi. New Delhi: Brijbasi.

Bercholz, Samuel, and Sherab Kohn, eds. 1993. *Entering the Stream*. Boston: Shambhala.

Beyer, Stephan. 1973. *The Cult of Tārā: Magic and Ritual in Tibet*. Berkeley: University of California Press.

———. 1974. *The Buddhist Experience: Sources and Interpretations*. Belmont, Calif.: Dickenson.

Bharati, Agehananda. 1970. *The Tantric Tradition*. Garden City, N.Y.: Doubleday.

Bhattacharyya, Narendra Nath. 1982. *History of the Tantric Religion*. New Delhi: Manohar.

Bubenik, Vit. 1996. *The Structure and Development of Middle Indo-Aryan Dialects*. Delhi: Motilal Banarsidass.

Cabezón, José Ignacio, and Roger R. Jackson, eds. 1996. *Tibetan Literature: Studies in Genre*. Ithaca, N.Y.: Snow Lion.

Chan, Wing-Tsit, ed. 1963. *A Source Book in Chinese Philosophy*. Princeton: Princeton University Press.

Chang, Garma C. C., trans. and annot. 1963. *Teachings of Tibetan Yoga*. Secaucus, N.J.: Citadel Press.

———, trans. [1962] 1989. *The Hundred Thousand Songs of Milarepa*. 2 vols. Boston: Shambhala.

Chitre, Dilip, trans. 1991. *Says Tuka: Selected Poetry of Tukaram*. New York: Penguin.

Cleary, Thomas, trans. 1998. *The Ecstasy of Enlightenment: Teachings of Natural Tantra*. York Beach, Me.: Samuel Weiser.

Conze, Edward, ed. 1954. *Buddhist Thought Through the Ages*. New York: Harper and Row.

———, trans. 1958. *Buddhist Wisdom Books*. London: Allen and Unwin.

Cozort, Daniel. 1986. *Highest Yoga Tantra*. Ithaca, N.Y.: Snow Lion.

Das, Sarat Chandra. [1902] 1979. *A Tibetan-English Dictionary*. Reprint. Kyoto: Rinsen Book.

Dasgupta, S. B. [1969] 1976. *Obscure Religious Cults.* 3rd ed. Calcutta: Firma KLM.
Davidson, Ronald M. 2002a. *Indian Esoteric Buddhism: A Social History of the Tantric Movement.* New York: Columbia University Press.
———. 2002b. Reframing *Sahaja*: Genre, Representation, Ritual and Lineage. *Journal of Indian Philosophy* 30: 45–83.
De, B. 1993. The Language of the *Dohā* and *Caryāgīti.* In *Aspects of Buddhist Sanskrit (Proceedings of the International Symposium on the Language of Sanskrit Buddhist Texts, October 1–5, 1991),* edited by Kamaleshwar Nath Mishra. Sarnath, India: Central Institute of Higher Tibetan Studies.
Dhammakaya Foundation. 1994. *Buddhism into the Year 2000.* Los Angeles: Dhammakaya Foundation.
Dimock, Edward. 1989. *The Place of the Hidden Moon: Erotic Mysticism in the Vaiṣṇava-sahajiyā Cult of Bengal.* Chicago: University of Chicago Press.
———, and Denise Levertov, trans. 1967. *In Praise of Krishna: Songs from the Bengali.* Chicago: University of Chicago Press.
———, A. K. Ramanujan, and Edwin Gerow. 1974. *The Literatures of India: An Introduction.* Chicago: University of Chicago Press.
Dowman, Keith. 1985. *Masters of Mahāmudrā: Songs and Histories of the Eighty-Four Buddhist Siddhas.* Albany: State University of New York Press.
Dudjom, Rinpoche. 1991. *The Nyingma School of Tibetan Buddhism: Its Fundamentals and History.* Translated and edited by Gyurme Dorje in collaboration with Matthew Kapstein. 2 vols. Boston: Wisdom.
Egyed, Alice. 1984. *The Eighty-Four Siddhas: A Tibetan Blockprint from Mongolia.* Budapest: Akadémiai Kiadó.
Eliade, Mircea. 1969. *Yoga: Immortality and Freedom.* Princeton: Princeton University Press.
Elias, Jamal J., trans. 1998. *Death Before Dying: The Sufi Poems of Sultan Bahu.* Berkeley: University of California Press.
English, Elizabeth. 2002. *Vajrayoginī: Her Visualizations, Rituals, and Forms.* Studies in Indian and Tibetan Buddhism. Boston: Wisdom.
Farrow, G. W., and I. Menon, eds. and trans. 1992. *The Concealed Essence of the Hevajra Tantra, with the Commentary Yogaratnamālā.* Delhi: Motilal Banarsidass.
Gellner, David N. 1992. *Monk, Householder, Tantric Priest: Newar Buddhism and Its Hierarchy of Ritual.* Cambridge: Cambridge University Press.
George, Christopher, ed. and trans. 1974. *The Caṇḍamahāroṣaṇa Tantra, Chapters I–VIII.* New Haven, Conn.: American Oriental Society.
Gethin, Rupert. 1998. *The Foundations of Buddhism.* New York: Oxford University Press.
Ghosal, S. N. 1956. An Enquiry into Eastern Apabhraṃśa. *Journal of the Asiatic Society—Letters* 22, 1:1–21.
Guenther, Herbert V. 1963. *The Life and Teaching of Nāropa.* New York: Oxford University Press.
———, trans. and annot. 1969. *The Royal Song of Saraha: A Study in the History of Buddhist Thought.* Seattle: University of Washington Press.
———. 1993. *Ecstatic Spontaneity: Saraha's Three Cycles of Dohā.* Nanzan Studies in Asian Religions 4. Berkeley: Asian Humanities Press.
Gyaltsen, Khenpo Könchog, trans. 1983. *The Garland of Mahamudra Practices.* Ithaca, N.Y.: Snow Lion.

———. 1990. *The Great Kagyu Masters: The Golden Lineage Treasury*. Edited by Victoria Huckenpahler. Ithaca, N.Y.: Snow Lion.

Gyatso, [Geshe] Kelsang. 1982. *Clear Light of Bliss: Mahamudra in Vajrayana Buddhism*. London: Wisdom.

———. 1991. *Guide to Dakini Land: A Commentary to the Highest Yoga Tantra Practice of Vajrayogini*. London: Tharpa.

———. 1994. *Tantric Grounds and Paths*. London: Tharpa.

Gyatso, Janet B. 1998. *Apparitions of the Self: The Secret Autobiographies of a Tibetan Visionary; A Translation and Study of Jigme Lingpa's* Dancing Moon in the Water *and* Ḍākki's Grand Secret-Talk. Princeton: Princeton University Press.

Hawley, John Stratton, and Mark Jurgensmeyer, trans. 1988. *Songs of the Saints of India*. New York: Oxford University Press.

Hess, Linda, and Shukdev Singh, trans. 1983. *The Bījak of Kabir*. San Francisco: North Point Press.

Hillyer, Robert Silliman, ed. 1941. *The Complete Poetry and Selected Prose of John Donne and The Complete Poetry of William Blake*. New York: Modern Library.

Hookham, S. K. 1991. *The Buddha Within: Tathagatagarbha Doctrine According to the Shentong Interpretation of the Ratnagotravibhaga*. SUNY Series in Buddhist Studies. Albany: State University of New York Press.

Jackson, David P. 1994. *Enlightenment by a Single Means: Tibetan Controversies on the "Self-Sufficient White Remedy."* Beiträge zur Kultur- und Geistesgeschichte Asiens nr. 12. Vienna: Verlag der Österreichischen Akademie der Wissenschaften.

Jackson, Roger R. 1992. Ambiguous Sexuality: Imagery and Interpretation in Tantric Buddhism. *Religion* 22: 85–100.

———. 1994. Guenther's Saraha: A Detailed Review of *Ecstatic Spontaneity*. *Journal of the International Association of Buddhist Studies* 17, 2: 111–143.

———. 1996a. No/Responsibility: Saraha, "Siddha Ethics" and the Transcendency Thesis. In *Felicitation Volume on the Occasion of the Sixtieth Birthday of H.H. the Dalai Lama*, edited by S. S. Bahulkar and N. Samten, 79–110. India: Central Institute of Higher Tibetan Studies.

———. 1996b. "Poetry" in Tibet: *Glu, mGur, sNyan ngag* and "Songs of Experience." In *Tibetan Literature: Studies in Genre,* edited by José Ignacio Cabezón and Roger R. Jackson, 368–392. Ithaca, N.Y.: Snow Lion.

Jinpa, Thubten and Jaś Elsner, trans. 2000. *Songs of Spiritual Experience: Tibetan Buddhist Poems of Insight and Awakening*. Boston: Shambhala.

Kapstein, Matthew T. 2000. King Kuñji's Banquet. In *Tantra in Practice,* edited by David Gordon White, 52–71. Princeton Readings in Religion, edited by Donald S. Lopez, Jr. Princeton: Princeton University Press.

Karmay, Samten Gyaltsen. 1988. *The Great Perfection: A Philosophical and Meditative Teaching of Tibetan Buddhism*. Leiden: Brill.

Kinsley, David. 1997. *Tantric Visions of the Divine Feminine: The Ten Mahāvidyās*. Berkeley: University of California Press.

Kunga Rinpoche, Lama, and Brian Cutillo, trans. [1978] 1995. *Drinking the Mountain Stream: Songs of Tibet's Beloved Saint, Milarepa*. Boston: Wisdom.

Kvaerne, Per. 1975. On the Concept of Sahaja in Indian Buddhist Tantric Literature. *Temenos* 11: 88–135.

———, ed. and trans. 1977. *An Anthology of Buddhist Tantric Songs: A Study of the Caryāgīti.* Oslo: Universitetsforlaget.

Lessing, F. D., and Alex Wayman, eds. and trans. 1978. *Introduction to the Buddhist Tantric Systems.* 2nd ed. Delhi: Motilal Banarsidass.

Lewis, Todd T. 2000. *Popular Buddhist Texts from Nepal: Narratives and Rituals of Newar Buddhism.* SUNY Series in Buddhist Studies. Albany: State University of New York Press.

Lhalungpa, Lobsang, trans. [1977] 1986. *The Life of Milarepa.* Boston: Shambhala.

Lopez, Donald S., Jr., ed. 1997. *Religions of Tibet in Practice.* Princeton Readings in Religion. Princton: Princeton University Press.

Lorenzen, David N. 1972. *The Kāpālikas and Kālāmukhas: Two Lost Śaivite Sects.* Berkeley: University of California Press.

Martin, Dan. 1992. A Twefth-Century Tibetan Classic of Mahāmudrā: *The Path of Ultimate Profundity: The Great Seal Instructions of Zhang. Journal of the International Association of Buddhist Studies* 15, 2: 243–319.

Mayer, Robert. 1996. *A Scripture of the Ancient Tantra Collection: The Phur-bu bcu-gnyis.* Edinburgh: Kiscadale.

McDaniel, June. 1989. *The Madness of the Saints: Ecstatic Religion in Bengal.* Chicago: University of Chicago Press.

Mishra, Kamalakar. 1993. *Kashmir Śaivism: The Central Philosophy of Tantrism.* Portland, Ore.: Rudra Press.

Monier-Williams, M. [1899] 1974. *A Sanskrit-English Dictionary.* New ed. Reprint. Delhi: Motilal Banarsidass.

Mullin, Glenn H., trans. 1996. *Tsongkhapa's Six Yogas of Naropa.* Ithaca, N.Y.: Snow Lion.

———. 1997. *Readings on the Six Yogas of Naropa.* Ithaca, N.Y.: Snow Lion.

Nālandā Translation Committee, under the direction of Chögyam Trungpa, trans. 1980. *The Rain of Wisdom.* Boulder, Colo.: Shambhala.

———. 1982. *The Life of Marpa the Translator.* Boulder, Colo.: Prajñā Press.

———, 1997. The Life of Tilopa. In *Religions of Tibet in Practice,* edited by Donald S. Lopez, Jr., 137–156. Princeton Readings in Religion. Princeton: Princeton University Press.

Namgyal, Takpo Tashi. 1986. *Mahāmudrā: The Quintessence of Mind and Meditation.* Translated and annotated by Lobsang P. Lhalungpa. Boston: Shambhala.

Nara, Tsuyoshi. 1961. Study of Some Interesting Linguistic Forms in Saraha's Dohākoṣa (1). *Bulletin of the Philological Society of Calcutta* 2: 63–73.

1962. Study of Some Interesting Linguistic Forms in Saraha's Dohākoṣa (2). *Bulletin of the Philological Society of Calcutta* 2: 1–10.

Nara, Yasuaki. 1966. A Study of Citta and Manas in the Three Dohas of Saraha. *Bulletin of the Philological Society of Calcutta* 6: 52–65.

Newman, John Ronald. 1987. The Outer Wheel of Time: Vajrayāna Buddhist Cosmology in the Kālacakra Tantra. Ph.D. diss., University of Wisconsin–Madison.

———.2000. Vajrayoga in the Kālacakra Tantra. In *Tantra In Practice,* edited by David Gordon White 587–594. Princeton Readings in Religion, edited by Donald S. Lopez, Jr. Princeton: Princeton University Press.

Norbu, Chögyal Namkhai, and Adriano Clemente. 1999. *The Supreme Source: The Fundamental Tantra of the Dzogchen Semde, Kunjed Gyalpo.* Translated by Andrew Lukianowicz. Ithaca, N.Y.: Snow Lion.

Olivelle, Patrick, trans. 1992. *Samnyāsa Upanisads: Hindu Scriptures on Asceticism and Renunciation.* New York: Oxford University Press.

Pradhan, V. G., trans. 1967. *Jñāneśvarī.* Edited by H. M. Lambert. London: Allen and Unwin.

Rabten, Geshe. 1983. *Echoes of Voidness.* Translated by Stephen Batchelor. London: Wisdom.

Radhakrishnan, Sarvepalli, and Charles A. Moore, eds. and trans. 1957. *A Sourcebook in Indian Philosophy.* Princeton: Princeton University Press.

Rahula, Walpola. 1974. *What the Buddha Taught.* 2nd ed. New York: Grove Press.

Ray, Reginald. 1986. Mahāsiddhas. In *The Encyclopedia of Religion,* edited by Mircea Eliade, 9: 122–126. New York: Macmillan.

———. 2001. *Secret of the Vajra World: The Tantric Buddhism of Tibet.* Boston: Shambhala.

Robinson, James B., trans. 1979. *Buddha's Lions: The Lives of the Eighty-Four Siddhas.* Emeryville, Calif.: Dharma.

Ruegg, David Seyfort. 1963. The Jo nan pas: A School of Buddhist Ontologists According to the *Grub mtha šel gyi me long. Journal of the American Oriental Society* 83: 73–91.

———. 1969. *La Théorie du Tathāgatagarbha et du Gotra.* Paris: École Française d'Extreme Orient.

Saṃkr̥tyāyana, Rāhula. 1957. *Dohā-koś.* Patna, India: Rāṣṭr-bhāṣā Pariṣad.

Samuel, Geoffrey. 1993. *Civilized Shamans: Buddhism in Tibetan Societies.* Washington, D.C.: Smithsonian.

———. Hamish Gregor, and Elisabeth Stutchbury, eds. 1994. *Tantra and Popular Religion in Tibet.* Śata-Piṭaka series no. 376. New Delhi: International Academy of Indian Culture.

Sanderson, Alexis. 1988. Śaivism and Tantric Traditions. In *The World's Religions,* edited by Stewart Sutherland, Leslie Houlden, and Peter Clarke. 660–704. Boston: Hall.

———. 1994. Vajrayāna: Origin and Function. In *Buddhism into the Year 2000,* edited by Dhammakaya Foundation, 87–102. Los Angeles: Dhammakaya Foundation.

Śāstri, Haraprasād. 1916. *Hajār bacharer purāṇa bāṅgala bhāṣāy bauddh gān o dohā.* Calcutta: Baṅgiya Sāhitya Pariṣat.

Schaeffer, Kurtis Rice. 2000. Tales of the Great Brahmin: Creative Traditions of the Buddhist Poet-Saint Saraha. Ph.D. diss., Harvard University.

Schmid, Toni. 1958. *The Eighty-Five Siddhas.* Stockholm: Statens Etnografiska Museum.

Schomer, Karine. 1987. The *Dohā* as a Vehicle of Sant Teachings. In *The Sants: Studies in a Devotional Tradition of India,* edited by Karine Schomer and W. H. McLeod, 61–90. Delhi: Motilal Banarsidass.

———, and W. H. McLeod, eds. 1987. *The Sants: Studies in a Devotional Tradition of India.* Delhi: Motilal Banarsidass.

Sen, Nilratan. 1973. *Early Eastern New Indo-Aryan Versification.* Simla, India: Indian Institute of Advanced Study.

Sen, Subhadra Kumar. 1973. *Proto-New Indo-Aryan.* Calcutta: Eastern.

Shahidullah, M. 1928. *Chants mystiques de Kāṇha et de Saraha: Les Dohā-koṣa et les Caryā.* Paris: Adrien-Maisonneuve.

Shaw, Miranda. 1994. *Passionate Enlightenment: Women in Tantric Buddhism.* Princeton: Princeton University Press.

Shendge, Malati T. 1967. Śrīsahajasiddhi. *Indo-Iranian Journal* 10: 126–149.

Shibayama, Zenkei. 1974. *Zen Comments on the Mumonkan.* Translated by Sumiko Kudo. New York: Harper and Row.

Simmer-Brown, Judith. 2001. *Dakini's Warm Breath: The Feminine Principle in Tibetan Buddhism*. Boston: Shambhala.

Snellgrove, David L., trans. 1954. Saraha's Treasury of Songs. In *Buddhist Texts Through the Ages,* edited by Edward Conze, 224–239. New York: Harper and Row.

———, ed. 1959. *The Hevajra Tantra: A Critical Study*. 2 vols. London: Oxford University Press.

———. 1987. *Indo-Tibetan Buddhism*. 2 vols. Boston: Shambhala.

Stearns, Cyrus. 1999. *The Buddha from Dolpo: A Study of the Life and Thought of the Tibetan Master Dolpopa Sherab Gyaltsen*. SUNY Series in Buddhist Studies. Albany: State University of New York Press.

Suzuki, D. T., ed. 1957. *Tibetan Tripiṭaka, Peking Edition*. Tokyo: Tibetan Tripitaka Research Foundation.

Tagare, Ganesh Vasudev. [1943] 1987. *Historical Grammar of Apabhraṃśa*. Delhi: Motilal Banarsidass.

Templeman, David. 1994. Dohā, Vajragīti and Caryā Songs. In *Tantra and Popular Religion in Tibet,* edited by Geoffrey Samuel, Hamish Gregor, and Elisabeth Stutchbury. 15–38. Śata-Piṭaka series no. 376. New Delhi: International Academy of India Culture.

———, trans. 1983. [Tāranātha]. *The Seven Instruction Lineages: bKa' babs bdun ldan*. Dharamsala, India: Library of Tibetan Works and Archives.

———. 1989. *Tāranātha's Life of Kṛṣṇācārya/Kāṇha*. Dharamsala, India: Library of Tibetan Works and Archives.

Thaye, Jampa. 1990. *A Garland of Gold: The Early Kagyu Masters of India and Tibet*. Bristol U.K.: Ganesha Press.

Thondup [Rinpoche], Tulku. [1979] 1982. *Buddhist Civilization in Tibet*. Cambridge, Mass.: Maha Siddha Nyingmapa Center.

———, trans. 1989. *Buddha Mind: An Anthology of Longchen Rabjam's Writings on Dzogpa Chenpo,* edited by Harold Talbott. Ithaca, N.Y.: Snow Lion.

Thrangu Rinpoche, Ven. Khenchen. 1993. *The Spiritual Biographies of Tilopa and Gampopa*. Boulder, Colo.: Namo Buddha.

Thurman, Robert A. F. 1995. *Essential Tibetan Buddhism*. San Francisco: HarperSanFrancisco.

Tonkinson, Carole, ed. 1995. *Big Sky Mind: Buddhism and the Beat Generation*. New York: Riverhead Books.

Torricelli, Fabio. 1997. The Tanjur Text of Tilopa's Dohākoṣa. *Tibet Journal* 22: 35–57.

Trungpa, Chögyam. 1983. *First Thought, Best Thought: 108 Poems*. Boulder, Colo.: Shambhala.

Tsong-ka-pa. 1977. *The Tantra of Tibet: The Great Exposition of Secret Mantra*. Translated and edited by Jeffrey Hopkins. Wisdom of Tibet Series 3. London: Allen and Unwin.

Tsuda, Schiníchi, ed. and trans. 1974. *Saṃvarodaya Tantra, Selected Chapters*. Tokyo: Hokuseido Press.

Tucci, Giuseppe. 1930. Animadversiones Indicae. *Journal of the Asiatic Society of Bengal,* n.s. 26: 125–158.

Urban, Hugh B. 2001. *Songs of Ecstasy: Tantric and Devotional Songs from Colonial Bengal*. Oxford: Oxford University Press.

Wallace, Vesna A. 2000. *The Inner Kālacakratantra: A Buddhist Tantric View of the Individual*. Oxford: Oxford University Press.

Wayman, Alex. 1973. *The Buddhist Tantras: Light on Indo-Tibetan Esoterism*. New York: Samuel Weiser.

White, David Gordon. 1996. *The Alchemical Body: Siddha Traditions in Medieval India.* Chicago: University of Chicago Press.

———, ed. 2000. *Tantra in Practice.* Princeton Readings in Religion, edited by Donald S. Lopez, Jr. Princeton: Princeton University Press.

———, ed. 2003. *Kiss of the Yoginī: "Tantric Sex" in its South Asian Contexts,* Chicago: University of Chicago Press.

Williams, Paul. 1989. *Mahāyāna Buddhism: The Doctrinal Foundations.* London: Routledge.

———, with Anthony Tribe. 2000. *Buddhist Thought: A Complete Introduction to the Indian Tradition.* London: Routledge.

Willis, Janice D., ed. 1989. *Feminine Ground: Essays on Women and Tibet.* Ithaca, N.Y.: Snow Lion.

Index

An italicized page number after a main entry indicates the presence of that term (or its unindexed verbal or adjectival form or synonym) in a dohā of Saraha, Kāṇha, or Tilopa.

emptiness (*continued*)
symbolized by female, 100, 101, 102, 104, 127, 145–146n25
in tantric practice, 22, 23, 32–33, 35, 36, 72, 73, 75, 88, 105, 106, 119, 137, 140
as tree, 41, 114
energies (*prāṇa*), 13, 33, 34, 35, 36, 63, 66, 75, 105, 119, 126, 127, 137, 138. *See also* breath; subtle body; winds
energies, five, 126
energy, 46, 144–145n17
enjoyment, 18, 26, 27, 63, 66, 85, 90, 93, 107. *See also* pleasure
enlightenment, 13, 14, 17, 18, 21, 25, 26, 27, 28, 30, 31, 34, 35, 36, 37, 61, 62, 74, 93, 104, 108, 112, 114, 118, 121, 127. *See also* awakening; freedom; mind: enlightened
error, 24, 31, 46, *54*, *65*, *67*, *88*, *89*, *96*, 109. *See also* ignorance
ethics, 27, 72, 120. *See also* action; Buddhism: ethics of; Kāṇha: ethics of; *karma*; Saraha: ethics of; Tilopa: ethics of; virtue
evaṃ, 32, 41, 118
evaṃkāra, *118*, *124*
evil, 46, *108*, 124. *See also* bad; vice
existence, 27, 28, 54, *61*, *65*, *66*, *67*, *69*, *73*, *79*, *83*, *86*, *88*, *89*, *110*, *112*, *115*, *124*, *129*, *132*, *135*, *137*. *See also* saṃsāra; triple world
and nirvāṇa, 28, 61, 67, 73, 86, 110, 112, 115, 124, 137 (*see also* nirvāṇa)
and nothingness, 21, 22, 31, 68, 69, 83, 88, 129, 132 (*see also* nothingness)

female, 15, 26, 94, 121, 123. *See also* action seal; mistress; woman
deity as, 11, 12, 32, 67, 100, 109, 123 (*see also* yoginī; ḍākinī; goddess)
symbolism of, 12, 34, 35, 63, 81, 100, 101, 102, 104, 127, 145–146n25
as teacher, 5, 7, 8, 15, 40
fields (sensory), 26, *106*, *129*
fire, 6, *53*, 59, *75*, *102*, 106, 119, *120*
fire of time, *121*
flower (as symbol), 17, 47, *114*, *118*, *134*
form, 16, 17, 67, *71*, 82, 93, *95*, *97*, *100*, 104, 105, 119, *120*, *139*
formless God, 44
fourteenth stage, *104*
fourth (as highest level), 34, *58*, 108
freedom, 14, 17, 18, 20, 24, 26, 28, 29, 30, 34, 37, 55, *56*, *60*, *61*, *62*, *63*, *67*, *69*, 72, *73*, *74*, *77*, *78*, 79, *88*, *90*, *100*, *104*, *109*, *110*, *115*, *123*, 127, *132*, *136*. *See also* enlightenment; nirvāṇa
fruit (as symbol), 17, 22, 30, 38, *114*, *115*, *117*, 127, *130*, *131*, *134*, 140

Gampopa, 8
gaṇacakra. *See* tantra: ritual feast in
Ganges river, 33, *80*
Garab Dorje, 5
Gateless Gate, 16
Gelug, 5, 11
gem (as symbol), 21, 22, 33, *73*, *96*, *122*, *124*, *128*, *138*
generation stage. *See* Yoginī tantras: generation stage of
generosity, 26
Ginsberg, Allen, 43
gnosis, 12, 13, 18, 22, 23, 34, 35, 36, 59, 63, 66, *76*, 95, 100, 101, 105, 108, 118, 119, 121, 122, 127, 128, 137, 140, 145–146n25. *See also* innate; wisdom
god, 22, 31, 44, 45, 46, 47, 67, *91*, *99*, *105*, 117, *119*, *136*, 145n17. *See also* utmost power
goddess, 32, 67, 100, 102, *123*, 127. *See also* yoginī; ḍākinī
good, 17, 22, 46, 47, 54, 65, *77*, *114*, 120, *123*, *134*. *See also* right; proper; virtue
grace, 4, 38, *107*
great bliss, 12, 21, 22, 23, 27, 35, *64*, *67*, *68*, *75*, *76*, 84, *96*, *97*, *105*, *108*, *109*, *118*, 119, *126*, 128, 137. *See also* bliss; ecstasy
great perfection, 5, 11, 146n28
great seal, 7, 8, 12, 21, 42, 76, 109, 127, *140*, 143n7, 146n28
Guenther, Herbert V., 50, 143n7
Guhyamantrayāna, 60
Guhyasamāja Tantra, 11, 12
guru, 7, 16, 22, 43, 45, 50, *62*, *63*, *68*, *69*, *71*, *72*, 79, *83*, *84*, *85*, *87*, *90*, *91*, *93*, *106*, *107*, *111*, *130*, *131*, *138*, *139*, *140*. *See also* master
blessings of, 4, 28, 37, 107, 131
definition of, 37–38, 62
ethics of, 37, 39–40, 72, 79
as human being, 40
importance of, 15, 17, 27, 36, 37–40, 44,

object (epistemic), 23, 27, 59, 62, 69, 74, *92*, *106*, 111, *130*, *133*, *139*. *See also* subject
offerings (ritual), 6, 13, 19, 20, 44, *53*, *60*, 63, *127*. *See also* ritual
omniscience, 23, *90*, 128
oneness (of reality), *67*, 84, 95, 98, *99*, 100, *105*, 110, *115*, *120*, 121, *126*, 139. *See also* sameness
Oriya language, 9
outcaste, 82, *85*. *See also* śūdra; untouchable

Padmasambhava, 5
Pāla dynasty, 6
Pāli langauge, 9, 22, 57
Panchen Lama (first), 5, 42
pandits. *See* scholars
passion, 12, 26, 35, 47, 67, 74, *127*, *138*. *See also* attachment; desire
Paśupatas, 5
Patañjali, 6, 30
path, 11, 12, 13, 18, 20, 22, 25, 26, 28, 29, 30, 31, 36, 37, 38, 39, 42, *55*, 56, *61*, 71, 72, 78, 101, 105, 108, *122*, 126, 129, 140. *See also* Buddhism: paths in
  of liberation, 35
  of means, 35
paths, gradual and sudden, 108
Pema Karpo, 42
perfection, 22, 56, 104, 109, 123, 132, 133
Perfection of Wisdom, 16, 20, 59, 104
Perfection of Wisdom Sūtra in a Single Syllable, 104
performance songs, 7, 8, 10
Persia, 6
pilgrimage, 19, 20, 26, *60*, 80, *81*, *136*
pleasure, 3, 14, 23, 26, 35, 64, 65, 67, 87, 94, *114*, 125. *See also* enjoyment
Prākrits, 9
pratyekabuddha. *See* Buddha: solitary
Prayag, *80*
proper, 14, 35, 54, 72, *112* (*See also* good; right; virtue)
Punjabi language, 42
Purāṇas, *62*, *117*, *128*
purification, 19, 23, 34, 38, 60, *72*, 75, *93*, *109*, *112*, 120, *132*. *See also* mind: purification of; purity
purity, 19, 32, 53, *70*, *72*, 81, *82*, *93*, *97*, 100, *113*, *134*. *See also* ethics; mind: natural purity of
  of behavior, 13, 25, 72, 92
  of mind, 3, 12, 17, 18, 20, 22, 31, 34, 36, 63, 70, 72, 93, 112, 113, 118, 134
  of world, 93

Rabten, Geshe, 43
Ramānanda, 43
rapture, 21, 26, 35, 64, *87*, *89*, *107*, *119*, 120. *See also* bliss; ecstasy
Rasa siddhas, 5. *See also* alchemy
Ravidās, 42
rati. *See* rapture
real, the, 17, 21, 22, 23, 30, 38, 40, *56*, *58*, 62, *67*, *70*, *71*, *76*, 77, *82*, 83, *86*, 96, *98*, *111*, *130*, *131*
rebirth, 12, 13, 14, 25, 33, 39, *61*, 92. *See also* saṃsāra
right (moral), 27, *54*, *72*. *See also* good; proper; virtue
Rilke, Rainer Maria, 43
ritual (or rite), 3, 4, 6, 10, 13, 19, 20, 36, 41, 45, 53, 66, 100, 126, *127*, 140, 144–145n17. *See also* offerings
Rousseau, Jean-Jacques, 46

sahaja. *See* innate, the
Sahajayāna, 21
Sahajiyās, 21
saints, crazy, 87
Śaivism, 5, 54, 81, 87
sākhī, 9, 44
Śaktas, 5
Sakya, 5, 7, 11
Samādhirāja Sūtra, 75
samarasa. *See* tastes the same
sameness, 14, 54, *75*, *95*, *96*, *97*, *99*, *120*, *130*, *132*, *133*. *See also* oneness; tastes the same
Saṃkṛtyāyana, Rahula, 7, 48, 49, 50
saṃsāra, 13, 14, 15, 20, 22, 25, 27, 61, 65, 66, 67, 69, *71*, 73, 80, 86, *88*, *91*, 92, 96, *115*, 124, 129. *See also* bondage; existence; triple world
saṃsāra-nirvāṇa cosmology, 14
Saṃvarodaya Tantra, 10, 32, 50, 56, 58, 59, 61, 62, 63, 64, 66, 73, 81, 91, 106, 119, 123, 140, 146n32
saṅgha. *See* community
Sanskrit language, 4, 6, 7, 8, 9, 21, 32, 48, 89, 104, 112, 147n59
sants, 4, 43–44, 45

Tao, 16, 17
Tao Te-ching, 16
Taoism, 6, 16, 17
tastes the same, 21, *76*, *80*, *95*, *123*, *128*, *129*. *See also* sameness
tathāgata. *See* Thus Gone, the
Tathāgatagarbha, 14, 22
tattva. *See* real, the
that (term for ultimate), 21, *62*
thought, 14, 17, 21, 22, 23, 24, 30, 31, 33, 35, 36, 37, 38, 45, 65, *66*, *68*, *69*, *70*, *72*, 73, *74*, *80*, *83*, *84*, *88*, *97*, *100*, *101*, *111*, *112*, *121*, *122*, *123*, *124*, *125*, *126*, *128*, *131*, *132*, *135*, *139*, *140*, *141*. *See also* awareness; mind; consciousness; intellect; nonthought
  conceptual. *See* mind: conceptual
  contrasted with mind, 65
Thus Gone, the, 21, 22, *123*
Tibet, 4, 5, 8, 11, 15, 22, 39, 42, 43, 59, 130
  Buddhism of, 5, 11, 28, 37, 43, 87, 108, 109, 140
  lineages in, 4, 5, 7, 8, 130
Tibetan language
  poetry in, 3–4, 42
  terminology of related to *Treasuries*, 22, 59, 75, 89, 92, 99, 107, 114, 136, 138
  versions of *Treasuries* in, 5, 7, 8, 10, 40, 48–50, 61, 66, 68, 85, 131, 134, 140, 143n7, 147n56, 147n59
Tilopa, 4, 6, 40, 42, 43, 45, 47, 63, 85, *131*, 144n10
  attitudes toward yoga of, 28–30, 137, 138, 140
  as cultural critic, 19–20, 131, 136
  descriptions of subtle body yoga by, 33–35, 122, 129, 130, 132, 133, 135, 137, 138, 140
  ethics of, 24–28, 129, 134, 136, 137, 139, 141
  focus on guru by, 37–40, 131, 138, 139, 140
  focus on innate by, 21–24, 129, 131, 132, 135, 136, 138, 139, 141
  historical uncertainties regarding, 7–8, 37
  in relation to females, 8, 15, 26, 35, 137, 138, 140, 145–146n25
  legends regarding, 8, 15–16, 40, 53
  meditation techniques in, 30–31, 130, 140, 141
  mentions of own name by, 131
  paradoxical rhetoric of, 16–19
  path proposed by, 35–37
  as practitioner of Yoginī tantras, 10–15, 29, 137, 140
  as progenitor of great seal traditions, 8, 41, 140
  as siddha, 4–5, 15–16
  as source of Tibetan traditions, 8, 39, 140
  Treasury of Couplets of, 8, 9, 10, 15, 16, 17, 28, 29, 41–42, 47–50, 129–141, 147n46
  view of body in, 24–28, 136
  view of mind in, 30–31, 130, 131, 132, 133, 134, 135, 137, 138, 139, 140, 141
  view of senses in, 24–28, 129, 130, 133
  view of sex in, 24–28, 34–35, 37, 137, 145–146n25
  works of, 8
titans, *119*
Torricelli, Fabio, 48, 49, 50
Treasuries of Couplets (as genre), 4, 9, 16, 27, 29, 42, 50
  commentaries on, 28, 48, 147n59
  differences among, 40–42
  editions of, 48, 147n56
  of Kāṇha (*see* Kāṇha, *Treasury of Couplets* of)
  language of, 9, 15
  provenance of, 9, 15
  redaction of, 10, 28, 29, 33, 39, 48
  of Saraha (*see* Saraha, *Treasury of Couplets* of)
  of Tilopa (*see* Tilopa, *Treasury of Couplets* of)
  translations of, v, 143nn7–8, 144n10
treatises, 6, 12, *62*, *92*, 104, *121*
tree (as symbol), 17, 22, 41, *114–115*, *134*
trimūrti, 82
triple world, 18, 23, 26, 30, 32, *67*, 82, *102*, *107*, *114*, *122*, *129*, *132*, *133*, *134*, *140*, *141*. *See also* existence; saṃsāra
Trungpa Rinpoche, Chögyam, 20, 43
Tsangpa Gyarepa, 42
Tsong Khapa, 42
Tukaram, 42
"Twenty-five Texts on Unthinking," 130

ultimate, the, 17, 21, 22, 23, 24, 26, 27, 28, 29, 30, 32, 37, 38, 43, 44, 59, 62, 64, 72, 77, 84, 87, *89*, 90, *117*, *128*, *131*, *139*. *See also* innate, the; real, the

ultimate (level), 16–17, 18, 22, 23, 24, 29, 33, 59, 63, 75, 77, 109, 111, 114, 135. *See also* conventional
unadorned, the, 18, 21, *117*, *134*, *135*
understanding, 18, 38, 71, 88, 107, *120*, *121*, 131. *See also* comprehension; knowledge
unthinking, 30, 41, *130*, *135*. *See also* mind: nonthought; nonconceptual
untouchable, *105*
Upaniṣads, 6, 16, 17, 23, 54, 58, 61, 114
  Saṃnyāsa, 6
upāya. *See* method
unstruck sound, 104, 105, 125
utmost power, 22, *87*, *100*, 120. *See also* god
Uttaratantra, 59

vajra, 22, 26, 88, 93, *107*, *128*
Vajradhāra, 128
vajragīti. *See* diamond songs
Vajrakīlaya Tantra, 11
Vajrapāṇi Tantra, 11
Vajrayāna, 11. *See also* Buddhism: tantric
Vajrayoginī, 11
Vedānta, 94
Vedas, 44, *53*, *103*, *117*, *128*
Venus, 32, *109*. *See also* Śukra
vice, 22, 27, *90*, *120*, *141*. *See also* bad; evil
Victor (epithet of Buddha), *124*
Vidyāpati, 42
Vimalamitra, 5
Vinaya, 57
virtue, 14, 22, 25, 26, 27, 38, *72*, *95*, *107*, *120*, *139*, *141*. *See also* good; proper; right
Virūpa, 5, 8
Viṣṇu, *82*, *136*
Viṣṇu Purāṇa, 62
visualization, 12, 18, 29, 31, 32, 58, 100, 122, 123, 127, 145n25
Voltaire, 46

water, 3, 22, 31, 44, *53*, 59, *60*, 68, *69*, 75, *77*, 80, *87*, *90*, *95*, *98*, *100*, *102*, *105*, *106*, *110*, *112*, *118*, *119*, *120*, *121*, *128*
White, David, 144–145n17
Whitman, Walt, 43
wife, 26, 39, *63*. *See also* mistress
winds (in subtle body), 12, 30, *75*, *119*. *See also* breath; energies
wisdom, 12, 14, 16, 21, 25, 27, 28, 29, 36, 50, *56*, 59, 61, 63, 65, 86, 93, 101, 107, 119, 127, 136, *137*, 145–146n25. *See also* Perfection of Wisdom; gnosis; insight
woman, 3, 4, 8, 26, 47, 63, 100, *137*, *138*, 145–146n25. *See also* female
word, 22, 38, 44, 45, *58*, *63*, *64*, *69*, *87*, *103*, *131*. *See also* speech; syllable
wrath, 12, 32, 46, *123*. *See also* anger

Yamāri Tantra, 11
Yamuna river, 33, 80
yoga, 5, 11, 13, 14, 15, 16, 24, 28–30, 33, 34–35, 36, 37, 45, 63, 66, 75, 76, 79, 82, 87, 91, 93, 105, 107, 121, 122, 125, 126, 127, 133, 137, 138, 140
Yoga Sūtra, 6, 30
Yogācāra, 7, 14, 69, 95. *See also* Cittamātra
yogas, four (of great seal), 76
yogin, 3, 4, 6, 27, 29, 32, 33, 42, 45, *55*, 63, *69*, *77*, *79*, 87, *90*, *91*, 93, *101*, *110*, *111*, *137*, *138*
yoginī, 4, 12, 15, 21, 26, 30, 31, 35, 39, 41, 100, *101*, *102*, 104, 109, 123, 127. *See also* ḍākinī; female
Yoginī tantras, 15, 21, 23, 25, 26, 32, 50, 58, 63, 67, 81, 144n16
  alternative names for, 144n16
  completion stage of, 11–12, 30, 33–35, 107, 118, 137, 140
  defined, 5, 9–15
  distinctive practices of, 12
  female imagery in, 12, 50, 67, 123, 137, 140
  four initiations into, 34, 58, 118
  generation stage of, 12, 31–33, 58, 88, 106, 109, 120, 123, 127
  in India, 10–11
  in relation to basic Buddhism, 14
  in relation to Hinduism, 14, 81
  in relation to Mahāyāna Buddhism, 13–14
  in relation to other Buddhist tantras, 12–13
  in Tibet, 11–12
  sexual practices in, 5, 12, 13, 16, 24, 26–27, 29, 30, 32, 34–35, 36, 37, 63, 64, 87, 105, 107, 109, 126, 127, 137, 138, 140, 145–146n25
  siddhas as practitioners of, 7, 15, 29, 50